Stories of Remembrance & Restoration: 100 Years of the Western District of the General Conference Mennonite Church

Edited by Loris Habegger

Wordsworth–Newton, Kansas

Copyright © 1992 by the Western District Conference
of the General Conference Mennonite Church

Published by Wordsworth, 702 N.E. 24th Street, Newton, Kansas, 67114

All rights reserved.

No part of this book may be reprinted or copied in any form without written permission, except in the case of brief quotations in critical articles or reviews, or for educational purposes.

ISBN 0-945530-08-0

Library of Congress No. 92-62070

Cover by Steve Banman

Computer typeset by Wordsworth

Printed in U.S.A. by Pine Hill Press, Freeman, South Dakota

DEDICATION

This book is dedicated to the people of the Western District Conference of the General Conference Mennonite Church who lived and witnessed to make one hundred years a time of praise and glory to the God and Father of our Lord Jesus Christ.

FOREWORD

During its centennial celebration year (1991-92), Western District Conference called upon a number of persons to help recall, through the medium of stories, 100 years of God's providence and leading. Throughout the district, audiences have been delighted and challenged by stories of persons, events, and movements that shaped its history and inform its future.

In the pages that follow, you will have opportunity to catch personal glimpses of leaders in mission and outreach activities, in educational and service institutions and programs, in congregational life and ministry, in establishing regional organizations, in planting new churches, and in controversial areas of the pacifist response to issues of war and peace.

At the time this book comes off the press, most of the persons about whom the stories are told and written have taken their places among the "cloud of witnesses." The storytellers are still among us and, even though the centennial year celebration has ended, many are still available to keep the oral tradition going; feel free to call upon one or more of them. We hope you will find pleasure and reward in reading and hearing these stories of ways in which God used extraordinarily ordinary persons over a period of 100 years to shape that part of the Christian family we know as the Western District Conference of the General Conference Mennonite Church.

—Patricia Shelly
Western District Moderator

—William R. Zuercher
Conference Administrator

PREFACE

A century is a small time fragment on the continuum of history. Yet generations living within a century accrue a remarkable residue of experience as they live through one hundred years. For the people of faith, time marks the continuation of the acts of God's people as they carry out the commission left to them by the Lord.

The Western District Conference of the General Conference Mennonite Church has now marked its first century of existence. It is time to remember the witness that has brought us to 1992. One way of remembering was initiated a year ago when the Centennial Committee elected to have storytellers travel through the many congregations of the district during this 1991-92 centennial year telling the stories of persons, institutions, and organizations as they have lived out their witness in our century of organized existence.

Many who have heard the stories have become interested in preserving them as the printed version of an oral tradition, imaging events and personalities that in time ahead become the history of our witness. This has prompted the Centennial Committee to venture the publication of the stories, intending that the storytelling will live on as their repetition renews us for the new century of witness to Jesus Christ that is before us.

This is a different book. It is neither formal research nor doctrinal directive. Rather, it is the gathering of stories to excite renewed interest, to encourage leisure reading, and to recapture through persons and exciting conference ventures the story of a century of witness to Jesus Christ, the Lord of the church.

Editing the manuscripts submitted by the storytellers has been a constant privilege. Every effort has been made to preserve the integrity and personalities of the storytellers just as they related their stories to numerous congregations. This should enable readers to read with the ear as well as the eye, indelibly impressing the stories upon us.

8 *Stories of Remembrance & Restoration*

Biographical stories include those of a cross section of conference witness—the well-known and the lesser-known. The stories will encourage further reading in the resources provided for those desiring more information. The stories are a tribute to God's people, those who have brought us to this juncture in history.

Thanks go to many who have been a part of the production of this book. The storytellers are commended for putting their efforts on paper as well as traveling and telling stories. Lorna Habegger Harder put in long hours entering manuscripts, where necessary, to computer diskette for editing and submission to the publisher. The publishing editor, LaVonne Godwin Platt, was ready and patient with assistance and counsel for final preparation of the pages of this book. Laura Cossey, Bethel College student intern with Wordsworth, gave skillful help in proofreading the manuscript. I thank Steve Banman who provided his expertise for the book cover design and photo layout suggestions.

Finally, an enthusiastic Centennial Committee provided the encouragement needed to enable final publication. These were Deb Ratzlaff, Lisa Janzen Scott, Marlene Krehbiel, Leann Toevs, Loris Habegger, James Juhnke, Wilma McKee, and Marlan Ratzlaff. The other members made chairing the committee a pleasure for me.

Hopefully, God will speak to you as you meet persons and experience the conference development through the stories. May we and our children after us become excited in the possibilities afforded by a new century which God places before us. The faith of our fathers lives on in the years ahead!

—Loris A. Habegger
Editor
October 23, 1992

Table of Contents

Foreword 5
Preface 7
Maria and Ursula van Beckum by Tim Lehman 11
Western District Conference Beginnings by Marlene Krehbiel 17
Oklahoma Convention Beginnings by Wilma McKee 25
Cornelius H. Wedel by David C. Wedel 33
David Goerz by David C. Wedel 39
Heinrich Daniel Penner by Maynard Shelly 45
Lester Hostetler by Maynard Shelly 53
Henry A. Fast by Maynard Shelly 61
Jacob G. Ewert by Bertha Fast Harder 69
Sister Frieda Kaufman by Bertha Fast Harder 77
"Creek John" Schrag by James C. Juhnke 85
Peter P. Wedel by David C. Wedel 91
Samuel S. Haury by James C. Juhnke 97
Jacob Reimer Duerksen by Lois Duerksen Deckert 103
Martha Richert Penner by Lois Duerksen Deckert 109
Mary Thiesen Goering by Marlene Krehbiel 115
Early Sunday School History by Rosella Wiens Regier 121
Church Planting Since the 1950s by Walt Neufeld 149
The Camp Mennoscah Story by Harley Stucky 161
Eden Mennonite Church of Inola, Oklahoma
                    by John W. Voth 175
Authors' Biographies 181

A Witness to be Remembered

MARIA AND URSULA VAN BECKUM

by Tim Lehman

Though the skies threatened rain, the embers still glowed with thin wisps of smoke rising heavily and low in the still air. The fires had been two, and the bodies of the martyrs now slumped charred and ghastly against the remains of their separate posts. Even as the last of the crows dispersed, the humid air held the lingering stench of burned flesh. The town was Delden, Netherlands, and even weeks later the bodies would continue their stench and decay for all the townsfolk to see and smell, a twisted reminder of Anabaptist resolve.

For now, though, the bodies lay there overheated and blackened beyond recognition, yet no stretch of the imagination could ever force the minds of the witnesses to forget the faces of Maria and Ursula van Beckum as they willingly testified to their faith even as the flames licked away their final breath. Maria had been taken first and they say that she went to the stake with a certain joy, proclaiming, "To thee, O Christ, I have given myself; I know that I shall live with Thee forever. Therefore, O God of heaven, into Thy hands do I commend my spirit." That face and those words are what the crowd left with that day. Though the authorities wished it otherwise, that horrible spectacle occuring the thirteenth day of November in the year 1544, only served to relive Christ's crucifixion in the minds of family and friends, only served to witness to a power far beyond the flames of fire or glint of steel-edged sword, only served to impress Maria's faith in like fashion deeper into the hearts of others.

Ursula, too, now had her rest. From the many efforts to cause her recantation, from the days and hours and minutes of awaiting the heated hearth of death, from the plague of heartsick love for husband, family, and friends, she was now released. Though her vitality could no longer be viewed from amid her earthly remains, the people knew. The eyes that had met her eyes were even now fully aware of the dancing light held in her soul. Though the fire had crackled and spit, Ursula's last words were heard and remembered above and beyond all images of death. As she mounted the altar piled there by the marriage of church and state, her foot slipped and the attending priest thought she might recant. But she said, "No, the block slips from under me; I will not faint in the Word of God, but constantly adhere to Christ." Ursula followed her sister-in-law, Maria, both of them now having had everything in life taken from them—yet not their faith, and not their love, and not their walk with God, and most certainly not their witness.

Perhaps it was the excitement in their voices as they told Maria of their baptisms, or their conviction as they told her how they had studied the scriptures, or their joy in newfound freedoms of personal faith shared within a community of believers—whatever the final reasons, Maria's life was forever changed as she stepped out in faith and joined the followers of David Joris. She had to leave her home, thrown out by her own mother because of her newfound faith. When Maria moved to the home of her brother, Jan van Beckum, even that was short-lived for she was hounded out by Goosen van Raesveldt who was the next in line to inherit Jan and Ursula's estate.

It was May then, and the still night air drifted easily with the smell of spring blossoms. The night air also held the hushed voices of armed men gathered around the van Beckum home while Goosen rapped loudly on the heavy wooden door. The clatter seemed to rattle the windows and it woke the van Beckums to a nightmare of violation, deceit, and heartache—literally a trial by fire. Maria had been found by her accusers, hunted down like an animal, captured as if in sport, and destined to live caged until death. But by God's grace she was not alone. Her sister-in-law, Ursula, had a love for her and a faith in God more powerful than any rabble with clubs led by a man filled with greed and sent by a church without God's love. That night both women were taken, bound together in love and willing to be friends in Christ even

Maria and Ursula van Beckum 13

unto death. Ursula by choice risked her own life so that she might accompany her frightened friend. Maria needed her, and Ursula also chose to spend the coming months in prison.

Did Ursula know on that still spring night that her friendship with Maria and her faith in God would take her to the stake? Could Maria have known that her request for Ursula's company would mean two martyrdoms, those two half-burned stakes and charred remains? Could anyone have guessed the terrible outcome of the warring madness of a dictated religion and the cruel deaths of many hundreds of Anabaptist martyrs?

Yet what has our story to tell us about six months of interrogation by priests and two women who witnessed unfailingly to their passion for life, friendship, and most of all, their commitment to Christ? What about their witness to those holding them at Deventer and then at Delden on November 13th, and what about their witness before all those gathered to watch their cruel sentence enacted in the flames?

As Maria and Ursula gave their final witness and bid each other their good-byes, many wept. According to tradition, Mennononites regularly planted a green branch on the site of Maria's execution well into the 19th century. Several Anabaptist hymns spoke the melody and the memory of Maria's faith and suffering.

These two courageous women, Maria and Ursula, were only two of some 278 women martyrs remembered in the *Martyr's Mirror*. *The Mennonite Encyclopedia* includes stories of some 525 early Anabaptist women. Together with the many men who joined them in bold witness to faith, often even in death, they have left us a call to faithfulness, a call to boldness, a call to resolve, a call to keep our eyes on God's incarnate way in this world, the emptying of Jesus Christ the servant, our Lord.

Is this witness, this boldness, the basis for the beginning and the future of Western District Conference? Have those who have gone before, gone by way of the flames, have they invited us to their courage and their witness? Of course they have! So will our every endeavor, every speech, be done in Christ's name and risk Christ's death in a society which still claims allegiance to other

14 *Stories of Remembrance & Restoration*

things? How will our witness be remembered 448 years from today?

It is raining now and none remain to gaze stricken mute at the bodies crumpled on coals now wetted and cool. But Maria and Ursula remain. They live in our hearts and our spirits, because their joy, even in death, is the story of our continuing life!

RESOURCES:

Jackson, Dave and Neta. 1989. *On Fire for Christ.* Scottdale, PA: Herald Press. pp 62-69.

The Mennonite Encyclopedia, Vol I. 1956. Scottdale, PA: Herald Press. p. 260.

Sprunger, Keith L. 1985. God's Powerful Army of the Weak: Anabaptist Women of the Radical Reformation. pp 46-47. *In*: Graves, Richard L (ed.). *Triumph Over Silence: Women in Protestant History.* Westport, CT: Greenwood Press.

van Braght, Thieleman J. *Martyr's Mirror,* 3rd English ed. Scottdale, PA: Herald Press. pp 467-468.

I read it in the minutes

WESTERN DISTRICT CONFERENCE BEGINNINGS

by Marlene Krehbiel

The Western District Conference, as it is now known, began with a strong desire to carry out an effective educational program for the children of the Mennonites settling in Kansas. This prompted the early leaders and teachers to meet together to develop a plan. As a result, the Kansas Conference of Mennonites was organized. The first official meeting was held on December 14-15, 1877. Ten congregations sent delegates, including some delegates from the Mennonite Brethern churches who were also concerned about educating their children. The agenda items of the first meeting included educational matters (curriculum, textbooks, school districts, etc.)—establishing a secondary school primarily to train more teachers, provide songbooks, organize home and foreign missions, and provide relief for needy congregations. The minutes of this first conference and all others were published in the *Zur Heimat*, a German newspaper edited by David Goerz.

A year later, in 1878, Goerz was sent to the General Conference at Wadsworth, Ohio, to report what the Mennonites of Kansas were doing. The Conference was pleased about the work being done and affirmed its continuation. The large number of Mennonites in the Kansas area meant that sometime in the future a redistricting of the General Conference would be necessary. So in 1888, *eine Mittlere District Konferenz* and in 1891, *eine Westliche District Konferenz* were established. Three organizational meetings took place. The first was in Newton, Kansas, November 4 and 6, 1889; the second in Gnadenberg, Kansas, in 1890; and the third in Christian, Kansas, in 1891.

In Newton, Kansas, on October 26-27, 1892, the last Kansas Conference was held. It was the sixteenth session. Believing that it would close with this session, the delegates resolved that the old officers should continue in office. Resolutions were read and tabled until the question concerning dissolution had been decided. The main work of the Kansas Conference was educational. Bethel College had been established for higher education, and the German Teachers Association (organized since 1875) was in place to work with the needs of elementary and secondary education. A committee was elected with instructions to sell conference property until all debts had been paid. Two other resolutions were brought before the house.

> Resolution 22—Due to the kind declaration of the Western District Conference to undertake the work of the Kansas Conference, the Kansas Conference is now ready to transfer such work to that Conference.

> Resolution 23—The Kansas Conference adjourns until some suitable time during these conference days.—Later (a matter of hours): Through the officers of the Kansas Conference the Western District Conference is informed that it has undertaken the work of the Kansas Conference (WDC minutes).

Then they sang *Num ziehen wir in Frieden* (Now we pass on in peace).

The minutes of the newly formed Western District Conference began with this entry:

> On Thursday, October 27, 1892, at 2 o'clock in the afternoon, the first Western District Conference was opened. Scripture passages which were read at this occasion and made the subject of contemplation were Matthew 6: 19-24 ... as a word for the opening; and Luke 19: 13 ... as a text for the sermon.
> (WDC Minutes)

Nineteen churches were represented at the first conference: Hoffnungsfeld, Christian, Hillsboro, Johannestal II, Garden Township, Gnadenberg, Halstead, Swiss Church at Elbing, Emmaus,

> *Matthew 6: 19-24:*
> Lay not up for yourselves treasure upon earth, where moth and rust doth corrupt, and where thieves break through and steal: But lay up for yourselves treasures in heaven, where neither moth nor rust doth corrupt, and where thieves do not break through nor steal: For where your treasure is there will your heart be also. The light of the body is the eye: if therefore thine eye be single, the whole body shall be full of light. But if thine eye be evil, the whole body shall be full of darkness. If therefore the light that is in thee be darkness, how great is that darkness! No man can serve two masters: for either he will hate the one, and love the other; or else he will hold to the one, and despise the other. Ye cannot serve God and mammon.
>
> *Luke 19:13:*
> And he called his ten servants, and delivered them ten pounds and said unto them, "Occupy till I come."

Brudertal, Johannestal I, Pawnee Rock, Newton, Zion, Pretty Prairie, and Hoffnungsau.

Some of the first resolutions to come before the conference dealt with appointing a Program Committee by the chairman and maintaining the organizational officers until new ones could be elected later in the conference. Other resolutions read as follows:

> Resolution 3—The Conference wished to obtain a clear understanding as to why the Hoffnungsfeld Church, which is entitled to 5 votes, had itself represented by only 3. Thereupon Elder Stucky gave the explanation that a part of the church wished to take a proving attitude at first.
>
> —Not being in favor of such a divided attitude, the Conference made this statement: The Conference recognizes the Hoffnungsfeld Church as being represented with five votes. The two missing votes were by the Conference conferred upon Bro. Jakob Stucky.

Resolution 4—Bro. H. R. Voth called the attention of the Conference to the fact that the death of the wife of our President, Benjamin Harrison, had been publicly announced. In the face of this sad event, the Conference resolved to send the following telegram of sympathy to Washington:

> To General Harrison, President of the United States, Washington: The Western District Conference of the Mennonite Church respectfully tenders its heartfelt sympathy to you in your great loss.

Brother Abraham Quiring was requested to see to it that this telegram was dispatched (WDC minutes).

Because it was now time to close the afternoon meeting, the conference resolved,

> that instead of the evening worship service, as they are generally held during the meetings of the conference, to meet again as a Conference after an hour and a half. And so it happened that at 7:30 o'clock in the evening one was again actively at work" (WDC minutes).

During the evening session matters concerning the Continuation School (a high school/academy at Halstead, Kansas) were discussed and a resolution passed that after the 1892-93 school year the Conference would no longer carry on the Continuation School, and the Bethel College Association would take up the work and carry it on.

Among other items on the agenda were itinerant preaching and the work of J. R. Toews in Wichita; the election of a committee for Church Affairs and one for School and Educational Affairs. The election of conference officers brought the following results: David Goerz, Halstead, Kansas, president; W. J. Ewert, Hillsboro, Kansas, secretary; and Andreas Wiebe, Beatrice, Nebraska, treasurer.

After a short recess declared by the Western District Conference to give the Kansas Conference a final opportunity to conclude their affairs, further resolutions were made: one, to hold an additional closed meeting after the regular adjournment; two, to print 1000 copies of the constitution; and three, to enter the following three questions in the minutes.

    a. Does the prohibition of remarriage, according to Matthew 5:32 and 19:9 and also I. Corinthians 7:11 apply also to the innocent party of a marriage separated through adultery (fornication)?

    b. May a church admit and receive such persons who have made themselves guilty of adultery through a marriage according to Matthew. 5:32 and 19:9?

    c. What would the Western District Conference advise if persons who have been received in other Mennonite churches without having been baptized on confession of their faith now seek admission in our denomination?

The Conference then:
    adjourned and closed with a grateful lifting of the eyes to the giver of all good and perfect gifts. May His blessing rest on the Conference and on the conference endeavors."
                               Wm. J. Ewert, Sec.
                               Dietrich Gaeddert, Pres.
                               (WDC minutes)

Some of the observations I made while reading through and reflecting on the minutes of early conferences include:

* The minutes of the first WDC were 14 pages in length. The 1957 minutes were 128 pages long.

* Each year at the conference three questions were posed to be discussed and dealt with. Somewhere through these 100 years this practice has been dropped.

* Early conference leaders were very concerned about the affairs of the individual churches. The 15th Kansas Conference made this resolution, Point 20: "With the addition of 3 brethren, the officers of the Conference are to investigate cases of conference members who with their behavior might damage the reputation of the Conference, and if possible, set them in order" (WDC minutes, p. 9). According to record, voting privileges were withheld from churches until matters could be set aright.

* There was grave concern over abandoning the German language, not because of the language itself, but rather fear that, having learned and taught the faith in German, the faith might be lost in trying to teach it in a new language. It is also noted that a 4-6 week intense German language and Bible study held during early summer, was dropped, taking away a large percentage of the churches' opportunity to teach.

Let us continue to bear in mind the purpose of the WDC as written in the constitution:

Mutually to foster our Christian life, to be drawn closer together in the bond of love, to cultivate more intensively the unity of the spirit, and to put ourselves in a position more efficiently to care for the interests of the Kingdom of God.

The New Mennonite Frontier

OKLAHOMA CONVENTION BEGINNINGS

by Wilma McKee

OKLAHOMA—LAND OF THE RED PEOPLE—land of dust and drought—untamed wilderness land, fought over and coveted. Why would any one want to leave "civilization" to come to Oklahoma? But they came. Mennonite families came to Oklahoma Territory in the 1880s and 1890s by the hundreds. The move tore families and congregations apart and tested the young settlers severely. What were the problems they faced? Were they equipped to handle them? Why did they need to organize an Oklahoma Convention of Mennonites? Couldn't they have been content with belonging to the Western District Conference? Wouldn't a separate organization foster disunity?

Some early families in the 1880s came as teachers, missionaries, and workers among the Arapaho-Cheyenne Indians of Darlington, near El Reno. The first General Conference church in Oklahoma was Mennoville, organized in 1891 with the help of missionaries and teachers from Darlington. Indian missions laid the foundation for Mennonite migration to Oklahoma. However, it would be a mistake to say mission work was the only inspiration for the many who came in the 1890s.

Land was in short supply in Kansas. How could a people who revered property ownership and independence accept this situation? The families were usually young with the adults from 25 to 40 years of age. They were often poor and seeking better economic conditions. They did not come to escape persecution or to preserve their faith. They came with a sense of adventure, caught up in the westward movement to the last frontier. They came for land and economic stability.

Persons from four of the Oklahoma Mennonite congregations took part in land runs—Geary in the 1892 run, and Meno, Medford, and Deer Creek in the Cherokee Strip Run of 1893. Polish Mennonites (Meno) made up the largest single group in the Cherokee Strip Run. Cordell (Herold) members came from Turkestan and found that land in Kansas and Nebraska was already taken.

What did the Mennonites find when they arrived in Oklahoma Indian Territory? They found a land which was earlier a center of ancient Indian culture and the crossroads for early explorers. It had become the home of more than sixty Indian tribes who had forcibly been removed to make room for white settlers. Many thought of it as a "young" land, but its heritage covered thousands of years and many nationalities. It had been described a short fifty years before by Washington Irving as filled with roving war parties, wild horse herds, black bears, wolf packs, and buffalo herds—a pristine wilderness. Then came the greatest change—in 1887 the Santa Fe railroad extended its lines across Indian Territory, and the land rush was on. Continued land openings allowed settlement of the entire western half of the state.

How did these repeated openings affect the territory? It was changed forever. No longer a quiet wilderness, it became a coveted land. It was a "fought over" land, where civil suits abounded and decisions for right and wrong were hotly contested.

Over 10,000 people came in one single day on April 22, 1889. It was a day that divided history, a day when honesty was discouraged and dishonesty was encouraged, even though many were sincere and honest seekers.

In many "would be" cities, secret societies abounded and governed the claiming of lots with the gun enforcing their rights. Members of secret societies took oaths that they would determine who got land. Boomers were everywhere, saloons flourished, and land-hungry pioneers, gamblers, and hucksters were all armed. It was a wild event, and the government was unable to maintain control. Oklahoma was called the "Promised Land." One writer described it as a "giant Easter egg hunt." These new Pilgrims did not usually kneel and give thanks; they coveted and demanded.

They often stole and plundered. Indian Territory was a rendezvous for a vast number of criminals of every description. Though people were for the most part law-abiding, there was no adequate law.

Blanketed Indians on spotted ponies roamed over the prairies, unable to make sense of the happenings, while outlaws hid in the hills. Scattered efforts were made to help the Indians. In Darlington they were taught to make hay and care for livestock. Indians also took on some of the work of freighting and were successful at it. They were noted for their honesty.

What does this have to do with the young Mennonites who came to the new land? It is necessary for us to understand this traumatic experience in order to empathize with the Mennonite families scattered randomly over Oklahoma Territory. They came because of problems which seemed insurmountable, only to find that the move intensified and increased their troubles. Their faith was challenged. Because the move was not by community endeavor, they experienced the loss of identity with the larger Mennonite community. Their decisions to come were often marked by alienation and division. Many of them had joined Kansas congregations in the early 1890s, and now they joined other congregations within 10 or 15 years. Their new congregations were small, often under 30 members, and at first relationships were usually nonexistent. Cooperation was rare and clannishness abounded. Ethnic Mennonites were not prepared to work together. The small congregations were usually leaderless. Previous leaders were older and established and did not wish to join this adventurous move. The exception is Meno where Elder Johann Ratzlaff came with his congregation. Small congregations found themselves living among non-Mennonites who spoke a different language and whose lifestyles they did not understand. They were daily reminded that they were a minority.

This aloneness was accentuated by separation from relatives in Kansas and other states. Oklahoma Mennonites sometimes felt they were the poor relatives who had been left out of their share of land in states where other Mennonites lived in large "protected communities."

The picture is not complete without adding the grimness of the economic times. The Mennonites had to experiment in farming their raw, undeveloped land. It was not ideal for Turkey Red wheat. There were drought and crop failure. For several years, men returned to Kansas to work for wages or to borrow money from relatives. Some cut lumber and hauled it to El Reno and Kingfisher for shipping.

In Western District Conference minutes from 1895 to 1898 are reports of assistance of money, clothing, and seed oats given by the Committee for Poor Relief to Oklahoma Mennonite congregations.

Many gave up, sold their land for whatever they could get, and went in search of better opportunities. One man traded his land for a shotgun and went back to Kansas. Many families moved several times, with the result that community spirit was destroyed.

The situation in Oklahoma Territory did not go unnoticed. Leaders were called out of the small churches and they voiced their concerns. Kansas ministers and conference leaders were aware through reports of itinerant preachers and conference committees of the desperate needs in Oklahoma. There was a deep concern for the spiritual needs of the infant congregations.

One solution was to form a Local Conference of Mennonites in Oklahoma. This was accomplished on September 12, 1899, in the large mission house in Shelley, Oklahoma. Seventeen of the ninety persons present were from Kansas churches. Christian Krehbiel, Halstead, Kansas, was elected chairman and M. M. Horsch, Arapaho, secretary. Their goal was to find a way for Oklahoma congregations to develop closer ties with one another. The original five points included emphasis on worship, encouragement of pulpit exchange, protracted meetings, and itinerant preaching to isolated brothers and sisters.

A decision was made to continue the conference assembly annually and later the name was changed to Annual Convention of the Mennonites in Oklahoma.

Oklahoma Territory was first on the Western District agenda in the early years and leaders in Oklahoma were supportive of the

Western District Conference. Itinerant preachers traveled the entire land and were a source of influence and encouragement.

When we consider the setting in Oklahoma Territory during the period, we can better understand the topics which were presented and discussed at the fourth Oklahoma Convention in the First Mennonite Church, in Geary, Oklahoma, in 1903. Using the title "Our Special Beliefs," the convention discussed taking oaths, refusing to bear arms, authority in the church, tithing, and secret societies.

The work was difficult but experiences of community built relationships in home and neighboring congregations. Togetherness made living through the hard times possible.

We can look at negative facts and say that at present only 17 of the General Conference Mennonite Churches are active out of the 36 established. We can also look at positive images and say that the fact that a number of churches did survive the hardships is nothing less than a miracle. This is a tribute to leaders in Oklahoma and Kansas and to the Oklahoma Convention which bound them together in community and service. Most of all it happened because of the faithfulness of God, the leadership of the Holy Spirit, and the redeeming work of Jesus Christ through the years.

The goal of the Local Conference at its beginning was to develop ties between scattered congregations. The Convention has reached this goal, but the years have proven that it has been service projects which have best drawn the churches together in a common purpose. There is great diversity among the seventeen Oklahoma congregations, but this is overcome by an even stronger basic faith in one Lord and in a determination to serve in ways which honor Him.

RESOURCES:

Directory of Oklahoma, 1989-1990. *State Almanac.* The Oklahoma Department of Libraries.

Hoig, Stan. 1984. *The Oklahoma Land Rush of 1889.* Oklahoma City, OK: Oklahoma Historical Society.

McKee, Wilma, ed. 1988. *Growing Faith: General Conference Mennonites in Oklahoma.* Newton, KS: Faith and Life Press.

Morgan, Anne Hodges and Rennard Strickland, eds. 1987. *Oklahoma Memories.* Norman, OK: University of Oklahoma Press.

Oklahoma Convention Minutes.

Western District Conference Minutes.

Wise, LuCelia. *Oklahoma Blending of Many Cultures.* 1975. Pride Publishers.

Wright, Muriel H. 1976. The Oklahoma Series. *In*: George H. Shirk and Kenny A. Franks. *Mark of Heritage, Vol. II.* Oklahoma Historical Society.

Cornelius H. Wedel
Credit: Mennonite Library & Archives

Educator and Writer

CORNELIUS H. WEDEL

by David C. Wedel

Are all little boys the same or are they all different? It is soon evident that little boys are different from one another. Each little boy sooner or later begins to write his own story. Cornelius H. Wedel was once such a little boy. His parents strongly influenced him to become different from other little boys. His father was a minister and teacher who loved his little son and would often talk to him about serious things in life. He did this because Cornelius' mother died when Cornelius was still a small boy, and his father became both father and mother to this little son. One of Cornelius's relatives said that they hoped Cornelius would become a pious man when he grew up; his father (and earlier, his mother) tried to teach Cornelius to be deeply religious.

Cornelius was born in the village of Margenau in the Molotschna Colony in Russia on May 12, 1860. Early indications were that Cornelius was nearsighted which prevented his participation in many of the activities engaged in by the other boys his age.

He soon became interested in books because his father had a large library and he often saw his father read for long periods of time. He learned early to think about what he had been reading. Poor eyesight made farm work difficult. More and more he began to think of teaching or even of becoming a missionary.

He immigrated to the United States in 1874, with his parents. His parents, who had long been prominent in the church and were respected by everyone, joined the Aleanderwohl congregation in their move from the Ukraine to Kansas.

In school, Cornelius made rapid progress in all subjects, and at age sixteen he became a teacher in the German school where he earned $10 a month. He soon began to write German tracts and articles, some of which he sold to his friends. During this time, he also tried to master the English language. By age 21 he had succeeded in earning a teacher's certificate.

While teaching was exciting, he saw a larger world ahead so he spent a short time at the mission station in Darlington, Oklahoma. Here the dust from mission buildings under construction hurt his eyes so much he had to come home, though he was still interested in missions. This interest moved him to enroll in Mckendree College in Lebanon, Illinois, to prepare himself for mission work. Soon it became evident he would not be able to fulfill this dream because his poor eyesight would disqualify him for missionary service.

At the peak of his discouragement something very wonderful happened. His church sent him to Bloomfield, New Jersey, to study theology under G. C. Seibert. He was such an eager student that soon he could read the Gospel of John in Greek. Even so his college days were not all happy experiences. He ran out of money; he was sick with fever. He was disgusted with the way people lived without God. Yet he always found encouragement when he came home and could preach. The first time he preached in his home church he prayed fervently that God would bless his words.

How quickly the little boy Cornelius had become a man who must make lifelong decisions. Just how he had come to know Susie Richert who was assisting with the mission work in Darlington, we do not know. He developed a great love for her, and his engagement and marriage to her was an occasion for a fervent prayer of joy and thanksgiving.

Now what should he do with his life? Should he stay in Bloomfield where he had been invited to teach, or should he work in the Mennonite Church? He talked to a number of Mennonite leaders, especially to David Goerz. He prayed fervently that he might be led to do God's will. The decision did not come easily. Pastor H. Richert had written a letter inviting him to start a school in Emmental. Benjamin Ewert invited him to teach in a preparatory school in Halstead. David Goerz informed him that the Bethel College Board of Directors had selected him to teach theology at Bethel, though he had received a specific, personal call to become a missionary. He finally decided to accept a call to come to Halstead, Kansas as a teacher. He was also ordained as a minister in the Alexanderwhol Mennonite Church in 1890.

After serving the Halstead school for three years Cornelius had to make another serious decision. Not only was he called to teach at Bethel College but to serve as president of the new school. While he was interested primarily in teaching he saw that he could help a people to change their attitude toward education.

Traditionally, Mennonites were opposed to education because they had experienced so much state-controlled education, requiring obedience with no questions asked. As Bethel's first president he would be able to formulate the curriculum and lay the general plans for the college. By many visits to churches he not only gained the support of the people for the school but also gained greater cooperation from the various cultures of the early settlers for conference causes. He dispelled many unfavorable attitudes simply by what he was himself, a scholarly, educated and pious master-teacher.

As a scholar he saw that the new immigrants needed to know their own history, but they brought no books to their new country. He undertook to write four volumes of Mennonite history. To do this he traveled to Holland, Prussia, Russia, Bavaria, and Switzerland. Most other Mennonite histories had been brief. He saw the Mennonites as an unbroken succession in the apostolic church. He pictured Mennonites as followers of their Savior, Jesus Christ. He saw that young people needed counseling in the area of courtship and marriage and wrote a guide to help youth to a common ideal. In another book he gave the pioneers a system of ethics as followers of their Lord. He wrote interpretations of questions in the Catechism as another book. For many the Old Testament held many difficulties, so he wrote a book explaining difficult passages.

Besides publishing books through Bethel College, he authored 182 articles on various subjects which were sent out to the general public. These were always based on his writings on the Bible as a guide to life and conduct. Next to the Bible, he felt that church history showed how faith led to a victorious life. C. H. Wedel was such a popular teacher that ministers who had been his students quoted him in their sermons. Students kept extensive notes in courses taught by him which were later copied by some who could not attend Bethel College.

Suddenly all the activities of this busy man came to a halt when on a Palm Sunday, ten minutes into his sermon, he had to stop. He had an attack of severe pain and weakness. Soon a severe case of pneumonia and pleurisy placed him beyond medical aid. He departed this life on March 28, 1910.

David Goerz
Credit: Mennonite Library & Archives

Minister, Educator, Publisher

DAVID GOERZ

by David C. Wedel

Some people can imagine all kinds of things. Some, after thinking about them for a longer period of time, begin to do something and write history. David Goerz was such a man. He was a Mennonite pioneer, business executive, teacher, editor, surveyor, relief worker, minister, merchant, a family man, community leader, and above all a man of God.

David Goerz was born June 28, 1849, in Neubereslav, a village near Berdjansk, Russia. Early in life he became an eager student at the Orloff Vereinschule. His mother hoped he would become a teacher or minister. She did not have to wait long, because at the age of 18 David began to give private instruction to the children of Cornelius Janzen, the noted immigration worker, known as the Moses who helped Mennonites from Russia and Prussia to come to America.

As a young man, David Goerz dreamed about America. Through letters to his friend Bernhard Warkentin, who had gone to America, he became interested in immigration to America. He copied letters which were made available to persons who were interested in immigrating, informing them what would be needed by immigrants to a new country. He became so involved in the promises of a new country that, after his marriage to Helen Riesen, and soon after his 25th birthday, he and his bride left for the United States. They settled in the Summerfield, Illinois, area.

Once in America he wanted others to enjoy this new world, and he organized a relief agency called The Mennonite Board of Guardians, to help people who did not have finances for immigration.

Shortly, David dreamed about a new location farther west. In 1875, when a group of Mennonites from Summerfield moved to Halstead, Kansas, David and Helen joined them. Here he organized the first Mennonite Teacher's Conference. At the meeting to which ministers had been invited, a resolution was adopted which led to the formation of the Kansas Conference. This later became the Western District Conference. David served either as secretary or chairman of this conference for many years. The constitution of the Western District Conference adopted in 1896 was largely his creation. He served as conference trustee from 1887 until his health began to fail.

About three years after David Goerz came to Halstead he was called and ordained by the local congregation to be its minister. He gained a wide reputation as a minister not only for the content of the sermons but also because of his presentation. He was a good pastor who could enter into the life situations of his people.

David Goerz had more dreams. When a committee was formed to plan mission work he contributed greatly to setting up such plans. He published a periodical for the immigrants called *Zur Heimat*. Six years later this paper was merged with *Der Mennonitische Friedens Bote*, a publication put out by the Mennonite Eastern District Conference. The new publication was called *Der Christliche Bundesbote* and was published by the General Conference Mennonite Church.

David Goerz was closely connected with the founding of the Halstead Seminary, the institution which later became Bethel College. When the Church failed to finance this school Goerz thought of raising an endowment fund for its support.

At this point a new dream appeared. The Newton College Association made an offer to the Mennonites to establish a college in Newton, Kansas. A special conference was called to consider the offer but no definite decision could be reached. Goerz came to this conference prepared for almost any emergency. Would the conference accept the formation of a corporation which would assume all responsibility for the college? It did not take long for this plan to gain acceptance. Goerz had special support in this action by

Bernard Warkentin and J. J. Krehbiel. The new corporation formed a board of trustees to promote this plan. On October 12, 1888, 2,500 persons assembled to launch Bethel College, which has now completed more than 100 years of educational services. Goerz served as the first business manager and gathered money for its support, sometimes driving in snowstorms because then he could find people at home. When it became evident that girls would come to Bethel in increasing numbers the construction of a dormitory for them was necessary. Goerz turned to his good friend, Peter Jansen, and persuaded him to solicit a gift from Andrew Carnegie. After repeated appeals urged by Goerz, a contribution of $10,000 was received from the well known philanthropist.

David Goerz also served the Bethel College Church as minister. He built Goerz Hall (which later was used as a college dormitory) because he wanted the campus to be a beautiful place. He once made the comment that a church should some day be located just north of his home: "Hier soll noch einmal eine Kirche stehen." (That is the site of today's Bethel College Mennonite Church.)

Foreign and Home missions held great interest for this pioneer. In 1890 he read a paper at the conference in South Dakota in which he presented deaconess work as a part of home missions. No one else had thought that women could become so active in the work of God's kingdom. When Sister Frieda Kauffman presented herself as a candidate for the deaconess cause, he had a serious problem; he had just agreed to go to India to help distribute 8,000 bushels of donated grain and to investigate the possibility of carrying on mission work. He vowed that if he could return safely from this mission he would do all he could to establish deaconess work among the Mennonites. He found a good location for mission work in India at Champa, where missionary P. A. Penner undertook his ministry to lepers. Upon his return from India, Goerz turned his attention to the deaconess cause. The Board of Directors of Bethel College made arrangements for deaconess candidates to train at the Deaconess Hospital in Cincinnati, Ohio.

The Bethel Deaconess Hospital and Home Society was organized March 30, 1903. The hospital building was dedicated

June 11, 1908. At the dedication Sisters Frieda Kauffman, Catherine Voth, and Ida Epp were ordained as deaconesses.

David Goerz was a talented business man. He used his talents not only for his personal business ventures, but in 1880 he organized the Mennonite Mutual Fire Insurance Company to protect early pioneers from devastating prairie fires. He had an extensive library and was well read in literature and theology. His travels were mostly for business purposes. He loved music and often directed church and community choirs. He loved the chorals in *Gesangbuch mit Noten*. He had a prominent hand in the publication of the song book, *Kleine Liederschatz*, and at least one song in the *Gesang Buch mit Noten* was published under his name.

David Goerz came to be one of the most respected and well known men in the Mennonite church, but he was a lonely man. His dreams and ideas were often so far ahead of the times that people did not understand what he was trying to do. He had the patience to wait until people caught something of his vision. The word "defeat" had no place in his vocabulary. He remained a dreamer all his life, which ended May 7, 1914.

Heinrich Daniel Penner
Credit: Mennonite Library & Archives

Blindness with Sight

HEINRICH DANIEL PENNER, 1862-1933

by Maynard Shelly

Heinrich Daniel Penner caught a cold, a really bad cold. The cold went into his eyes. He lost the sight in one eye and could barely see out of the other. He had to drop out of school in the fall of 1880 when he was 18 years old. He never studied in a formal school again.

Heinrich's schoolteacher father died when Heinrich was nine years old. Three years later, in 1874, Heinrich left for Kansas with his mother and stepfather. His mother died four years after the family settled on a farm near Hillsboro. So, by age 16, he had no parents.

For two years before his vision loss, he attended Peter Balzer's school, the forerunner of Bethel College. By then he could barely see, but after a time his health improved as did the sight in one eye.

Painful events in 1932
In 1884, he married Katharina Dalke; she helped him become "physically well, mentally alert, and spiritually happy." Heinrich went on to become a teacher, the founder of the Penner Academy in Hillsboro, a professor at Bethel College, and a minister. He served as pastor to churches in Hillsboro; Beatrice, Nebraska; and Geary, Oklahoma. For a time, he was pastor at the Bethel College Church, chaplain at Bethel Hospital in Newton, and spiritual advisor for the deaconesses there. Active in the work of the Western District Conference, he served as General Conference president during the years around World War I.

Though he had sight in only one eye, he had the piercing vision of a prophet. Let's drop in on him in 1932 when he was 70 years old.

The action takes place in two scenes in the Newton City Auditorium. One happened in April and the other in October 1932. Penner may or may not have been at the April meeting that had to choose between the life and death of Bethel College. At the Western District meeting on October 20, Heinrich tried to be a peacemaker and took a beating for it.

The Newton City Auditorium stood at Sixth and Poplar Streets. People remember it as a large, dark-colored room, with galleries on three sides. It had the meanest folding chairs ever devised for human torture. But the seats cannot be blamed for the painful events that took place there.

Fire storm over Bethel
It was a dry year in 1932—a very dry year. It was so dry, that if you were afraid of fire, you were being careful. But Heinrich Daniel Penner struck a match.

President Herbert Hoover was running for reelection. A fellow from New York named Franklin Roosevelt was the Democrat running against the Republican Hoover. The *Mennonite Weekly Review* favored Hoover. He supported Prohibition. It forbade the sale of all alcoholic beverages. Democrats were promising to repeal prohibition and legalize the strong drink sales once more.

Bethel College, as usual, was in trouble. It was the height of the Fundamentalist/Modernist clash in Protestant churches. Fundamentalists were suspicious of higher education. After World War I, Mennonite leaders swayed by Fundamentalism attacked Bethel's teachers. "Let's have teachers who have answers, not just questions," they said. Penner was one of the professors caught in the fray. He quietly left the faculty in 1917, never to return to school teaching again.

In the 1930s, the attack on Bethel shifted. Now they said, "Let's have a different kind of school! Build a Bible school with teachers who have answers instead of questions! In January 1932, H. P. Krehbiel, editor of the *Mennonite Weekly Review,* called for a Bible school and assailed Bethel. "What a tragedy," he said. "Young people, brought up in Mennonite homes and communities, are robbed of their faith."

Krehbiel had already drawn up plans for a new school. He called it the Menno Christian Workers School.

Bethel College was strapped for cash in 1932. But the Western District had just raised $100,000 for its support. Some folks, including H. P. Krehbiel, wanted that money back to build their Bible school. President J. W. Kliewer said no. The money was raised for Bethel College. Yet the Bible school people insisted it was their money. They had given it.

So, a special meeting of the College corporation was called for April 6. H. C. Friesen from Buhler rose to complain about a Rev. Fred Smith of Newton, who had spoken at a recent peace conference held in the college chapel. "The speaker flatly denied the authority of the Bible. Does Bethel College still stand firmly on the Bible, on which she was founded, or has the work of undermining the foundation begun?"

Of course, Bethel had its defenders. They stood to be counted. The vote was taken: 149 to 131. A switch of ten votes might have doomed the college. Bethel had been spared from the fire.

Social gospel starts a riot
In October, the people of the Western District came back to the Newton Auditorium for their yearly meeting. Was all danger of fire past? No.

The major address was to be given by H. D. Penner who then was pastor of a church in Oklahoma. In his talk, Penner took hold of the ruckus between Fundamentalism and Modernism. He said both sides have a piece of the truth. Fundamentalists believe in conversion, often a crisis conversion. Personal commitment, said Penner, is important. That's what adult baptism is all about. Mennonites have always warmed to talk of conversion and personal religion.

But many Mennonites were drawn by the call of Protestant liberals to the social gospel. That meant living for Christ in service to the world. Such is the path of Christian discipleship.

Penner opened his Bible and went through the seven parables of Jesus in Matthew 13 one by one. "In one, Jesus speaks about personal religion; and in the next, he speaks about the social gospel," Penner said. The title for his address was "The Twofold Nature of the Kingdom."

Did he feel that he, at last, had solved the Fundamentalist/Modernist fight? Maybe. Did he win friends and influence people? He surely didn't. Almost at once, things began to fall apart in the Newton Auditorium.

Strike this speech from the record! Don't allow it to be published! Investigate this man who says these awful things!

That was the response from some. Penner thought he had proved from the Bible that Jesus stood for both personal conversion and for social gospel. But for people trained in the code language of Fundamentalism, anyone who praised the social gospel was a Modernist. If word got out that the social gospel had been lauded in the Newton City Auditorium, it would be a stain on the good Mennonite name.

Let's take a vote, they said. Let's show that "we believe that faith in Jesus Christ and his blood is the only way to forgiveness of sin."

Well, nothing of his sermon appeared in the minutes of the Western District. But Penner dug into his own pockets, printed his lecture, and sold it for ten cents a copy.

With sight in both eyes

Of course, Heinrich Penner felt that discipleship was important. He was seventy years old. Always bold, he was willing to take a risk. As the years went on, he had grown ever more daring.

Many would have said, "Keep quiet. Now's not the time to make people nervous." He was, I think, the apostle of lost causes. But he wouldn't agree. He saw himself as the apostle of God's rule.

One of the sore toes in the General Conference for many years had been the matter of lodge membership. The General Conference had opposed secret societies since its founding in 1860. But in 1926, at the conference in Berne, Indiana, Penner got up to say a good word for lodges. Sure, he was opposed to secrecy. But in their practice of mutual aid, the lodges were doing a Christlike thing. Did the leaders of the General Conference reward his courage? They did not. They refused to print his words in their minutes.

Heinrich Daniel Penner was a bit like Harry Emerson Fosdick. A minister in a New York Presbyterian Church in the 1920s, Fosdick was a preacher of discipleship and social gospel. Thus he got the reputation of being the country's number one Modernist —the man the Fundamentalists loved to hate. Many people, even Mennonites, saw Fosdick as a heretic. But others found him a daring crusader for the full gospel of Jesus Christ, a real evangelical.

In 1925, Fosdick preached a sermon in which he said, "I'm a heretic and I'm glad of it because Christ was a heretic too."

After hearing this, Penner said, "Wish we had more heretics of his type. The millennium would soon become a very present reality."

Heinrich Daniel Penner died in 1933 at the age of 71. Because of his handicap, he was denied many customary activities. He never learned how to drive a car, never even owned a car. Did his limited physical vision keep him from applying for a driver's license?

No matter. His vision of Jesus Christ was sharp and clear. He dared to say what he saw. He saw the church walking in the steps of Jesus Christ.

RESOURCES:

Krahn, Cornelius. 1956. *Mennonite Encyclopedia, Vol. IV.* Scottdale, PA: Mennonite Publishing House. pp. 134f.

Clarence B. Niles, 1975. *A Short Biography of My Grandfather, Heinrich Daniel Penner: Pioneer Mennonite Teacher and Minister.*

Jan Niles, 1978. *H. D. Penner and the Hillsboro Preparatory School*, unpublished manuscript.

H. D. Penner, 1932. *The Twofold Nature of the Kingdom According to the Seven Parables of Jesus in Matthew 13* (address given at the Western District Conference on October 20, 1932).

H. P. Peters, 1925. History and Development of Education Among the Mennonites of Kansas.

[Note: The Mennonite Library and Archives, North Newton, Kansas, contains H. D. Penner's personal papers, records, and other resources, including those listed above.]

Lester Hostetler
Credit: Mennonite Library & Archives

An Exile Ends in Song

LESTER HOSTETLER, 1892–1989

by Maynard Shelly

For Lester Hostetler, the Western District Conference was a land of exile, as events of his life will soon reveal. Gifted as a preacher, writer, and musician, he taught the church to sing wherever he went—California, Kansas, South Dakota, or Ohio.

It all started in Holmes County, Ohio, land of his birth, in the age-old family of Amish Mennonites. For 45 years, he carried the pain of being rejected by his kin. He was 32 years old in 1924 when cut off from the Eastern Amish Mennonite Conference.

The Amish nurture family feeling, guarding their traditions with care. Such are the ways of the Old Order as well as progressive groups like the Eastern Amish Mennonites. They built a church at Walnut Creek, Ohio, in 1862, 30 years before Lester Hostetler was born near Sugarcreek where his family helped form a branch congregation.

It was in Walnut Creek where he was ordained a minister in 1915. He had just graduated from Goshen College and was on his way to Union Theological Seminary in New York. Even among the progressive Amish, Lester was out in front. One of the first to go to college, he became the first minister of his conference to go to seminary.

Coming back to Ohio, he was eager to share all he had learned about the Bible and music. But not everyone greeted the future leader with open arms.

I wrote a letter to my love, and put it in a locket
In the summer of 1917, Lester was working on the family farm after finishing his second year at Union. He preached in both of

his home churches each Sunday. During the week, he taught music classes.

He and his Union classmates kept in touch during the summer with a round robin letter. When this packet with notes from each of his friends came to him, he quickly penned his report. While some of his friends found people opposed to what they felt was seminary heresy, Lester said the Amish in Ohio heard him without criticism. Although some ministers in his conference viewed his seminary training with an "evil eye," Lester felt sure of his ability to lead. "I have endeavored," he wrote, "to respect the faith and beliefs of the people."

I sent a letter to my love, and on the way he dropped it
Lester mailed the bundle on to A. P. Funkhouser, Harrisonburg, Virginia, the next student on the list. Funkhouser was not a Mennonite, but he lived among some who had just built Eastern Mennonite School on the north side of town. J. B. Smith, once a teacher at Hesston College in Kansas, had just become its first president. Smith was concerned about right doctrine. In the debates of the time, he was on the side of the fundamentalists eager to root out the poison of modernist teaching. Lester called Smith his "most aggressive adversary." In the letter he wrote that Smith "saw modernism as a threat to the church and was outspoken in his condemnation of schools he believed to be unorthodox."

When the round robin arrived in Harrisonburg, Funkhouser was ill. He could neither write nor send the letters on. In fact, that illness became his last and he died. In the course of time, Funkhouser's goods were put up for sale.

The one who picked it up, he used it like a rocket
J. B. Smith, a collector of religious books, came to the auction and bought some books and files. Leafing through the papers he had bought, he found the Union class letters. He thought them a gift from God. Lester Hostetler had indeed been corrupted by Union Seminary. He had, it seemed to Smith, admitted it in his own words.

Smith sent a copy of Lester's letter to every Mennonite minister in the United States. In his cover letter, Smith said Lester had shown himself as a "full fledged Union Seminary heretic." Such a person, Smith said, "should not only be silenced in the pulpit, but unless he repents, his name should not be tolerated on the roll of our beloved Church."

What a stir that letter caused everywhere! Yet the people at Walnut Creek and Sugarcreek who had known Lester from early childhood really had no problem. When he read the class letter at a midweek service, few could find anything wrong in it. Most said, "That sounds just like Lester." Even Daniel Kauffman, editor of the *Gospel Herald*, who agreed that Union was an unorthodox school, said Smith had done wrong by sending Lester's letter far and wide.

Smith's campaign, however, wounded the Mennonite Church as well as Lester. Though still a young man in the 1920s, Lester had been chosen to help prepare a new hymnal. He was a natural choice, for he had made a special study of church music in Union. When he became the target of controversy, Lester, as he would later say, was "unconsciously dropped." One member who continued on the committee that produced the *Church Hymnal* in 1927 was J. B. Smith.

While Smith's campaign could not force Lester from the Walnut Creek and Sugarcreek churches, the bishops could. They felt a need to maintain the form of the church they had received. Their image and the vision of the seminary-trained minister were bound to collide.

Welcomed home when he hadn't been away
Before Lester's second year at Union, the Amish Mennonite Conference met to consider a proposal forbidding members to attend Union Theological Seminary. Lester and his friends thought the idea silly. He felt sure the proposal would not carry, so he stood to vote no. Looking around, he found he was standing alone. It was his first, but not last, lesson about the power of the bishops.

In spite of this ban, Lester went back to Union, for he had really enjoyed his first year. He knew his teachers as sincere Christians who opened the Bible and the world to him. Besides, he was paying his own way along with the help of a seminary scholarship.

None of the bishops had ever been to a seminary. They were unsure how to deal with one who stirred the church to new ways of service. In those days, even Goshen College was under a cloud. People whispered about its teaching evolution. Having heard of heresy everywhere, the bishops linked Lester's name to their fears, and Lester had to be examined by them. They appointed a committee to explore his soundness. Of special weight in his favor was the testimony of Samuel H. Miller, the senior minister at Walnut Creek. He found much good in Lester's preaching. And Lester willingly subscribed to the doctrines of the church.

The investigators, like Pilate, reported that they found no fault in this man. He had answered their questions well. The bishops said they would receive him back as a minister in good standing.

Good news? Lester thought not. He had never been expelled, he said. His membership had never been revoked. His accusers were the ones who had given false testimony. They were the ones to be censured.

Bishops visit Sugarcreek once too often
Life at Walnut Creek and Sugarcreek was often mixed with strife. The issue of dress was a troubling one for the congregation. In 1922, a committee, including eight women, was appointed to study the matter. Conference leaders were pressing for conformity on the issue of nonconformity.

Since its beginnings in 1897, the Sugarcreek congregation had been a union church with the Church of the Brethren. Mennonites and Brethren had separate worship services, but they met together for Sunday school. In the spring of 1924, trouble came to Sugarcreek in the person of Bishop J. S. Gerig. He asked that the Mennonites have their own school to study Mennonite lessons. Without consulting Lester, Gerig went from house to house asking support for his idea. Lester opposed the plan. The congregation may not have liked the idea, but they thought they had no choice.

On Sunday, June 24, 1924, Lester resigned as the minister of both Sugarcreek and Walnut Creek. This is a large world, he said. He would look for another field where he could work without outside interference. He asked his friends to stay and work for unity from within.

Within days of his resignation, a committee of conference bishops, one of them from Pennsylvania and another from western Ohio, came to Walnut Creek. They had come to explain what the conference had against their minister. Since Lester had already resigned, all this was beside the point. All that remained to be done was to make sure that the people of Walnut Creek and Sugarcreek would vote to accept his resignation.

So the bishops moved to take a vote. It was not a secret ballot. It was a face-to-face roll call vote, with the bishops passing through the pews, asking each person, one by one, for his vote.

"Each member therefore would have to confront not only God and his conscience, before he voted," said Lester, "but also the bishop or minister taking the vote." The vote was amazingly close — 139 to 101. Lester Hostetler was no longer a minister in the Amish Mennonite Conference.

People from Sugarcreek asked Lester to form a congregation separate from Walnut Creek. It was a peaceful parting. In 1926, Sugarcreek joined the General Conference. And so Lester became a General Conference pastor at the age of 34, continuing his career as pastor and musician.

Lester came to Bethel College by way of Upland, California, in 1941, to become editor of the *Bethel College Bulletin*. In 1942, he became pastor of the Bethel College Mennonite Church, North Newton, Kansas. His special gifts to the wider church came in the *Youth Hymnary*, the *Handbook to the Mennonite Hymnary*, and the *Mennonite Hymnary* which he and Walter Hohmann co-edited. The 1940 *Hymnary* was well received. Paul Wohlgemuth in his doctoral thesis on hymnals called it "the best hymnal that the

General Conference Mennonites or any other Mennonite conference has published."

When the General Conference set out in the late 1950s to revise its 1940 hymnal, Lester was again on a hymnal committee. Now ready to redo its 1927 *Church Hymnal*, the Mennonite Church was open to working on a book to serve both denominations. As work advanced, Lester seemed the likely General Conference candidate for co-editor with Walter E. Yoder from the Mennonite Church. Lester could hardly believe it.

"We are working together now," he said. "But when this book comes out, you are surely not going to have my name on it as an editor?" He recalled how he had once been "kicked off" an earlier hymnal group.

"Yes, we are," said Chester K. Lehman, once dean of Eastern Mennonite School and member of the 1927 *Church Hymnal* committee. "That was long ago. This is a different time."

So, in 1969, when people in General Conference and Mennonite Church congregations including one in Walnut Creek, Ohio, opened the *Mennonite Hymnal* to sing the Lord's songs, a spiritual exile ended. Lester Hostetler had come home.

RESOURCES:

Lester Hostetler, 1980. *My Spiritual Pilgrimage*. unpublished autobiography, at Mennonite Library and Archives, North Newton, Kansas, and in Mennonite Historical Library, Goshen, Indiana.

James C. Juhnke, 1989. "The 1920s: Moving Forward and Holding Back," pp. 265-269 in *Vision, Doctrine, War (The Mennonite Experience in America, Vol. 3)*. Scottdale, PA: Herald Press.

Ervin Schlabach, 1981. *The Amish and Mennonites at Walnut Creek*. Millersburg, Ohio: 1981, pp. 81-96 [includes text of Hostetler's letter to his Union Seminary classmates in 1917 and J. B. Smith's interpretation of it].

J. Kevin Miller, 1990. "Lester Hostetler, 1892-1989: In Memoriam." *Mennonite Historical Bulletin,* April 1990.

Henry A. Fast
Credit: Mennonite Library & Archives

Pacifist with a Square Jaw

HENRY A. FAST, 1894-1990

by Maynard Shelly

It turned into a riot. In fact, it was a full-blown rebellion in a Mennonite community. The people in Downey, Idaho, rose up to tar and feather their leader. This Civilian Public Service camp in the early 1940s wasn't an ideal community. Here were a group of young men digging irrigation ditches far from home. In their stress and homesickness, they turned their anger on a camp director who found it hard to cope with an unfamiliar job.

When Henry A. Fast, administrator of Mennonite CPS camps, got the news, he made a quick trip to Idaho to restore order. Once in the camp, he called for the ringleader of the mutiny. Fast was standing as the burly fellow came into the room.

"Sit down," said Fast.

"I prefer to stand," said the defiant farm hand from Hillsboro, Kansas.

Fast responded sternly. "I said, <u>sit down</u>." Later, back home in Newton, Kansas, Fast told his wife, "I really don't know what I would have done if he hadn't."

Army officer curses way of peace
People of the Western District Conference looked to H. A. Fast as their leader in the way of peace. After all, he wrote the book called *Jesus and Human Conflict*. Based on his 1936 doctoral study at Hartford Theological Seminary on Jesus and nonviolence, it was a pioneer piece of research.

When it came to making the way of peace work, Henry Fast did it with passion and grit. With a touch of paternalism, he was our pacifist with the square jaw and our trailblazer in World War II.

His wake-up call came a year after he graduated from Bethel College. His draft board ordered him to report to Camp Funston in Kansas by May 23, 1918. The United States was embroiled in World War I. Henry was principal of the high school at Whitewater, Kansas, but had to leave a week before the term ended.

Mennonite leaders, unprepared for the draft, had advised their young men to report to army camp when called and there declare their objections to military service. Henry pondered this question on the train to camp: How should he confront the order to accept a gun and combat training?

At the desk in the large hall for recruits, he answered the routine questions. Then he asked the sergeant for an assignment to hospital work. He wanted this, he said, because "I am a conscientious objector." When the brawny man in uniform heard those words, he rose up in anger.

"Damn C.O.!" he said in his loudest voice. "Damn C.O.!"

Each person in that large room was jolted wide awake. Every head turned to see this odd fellow too cowardly to fight for his country.

Unpleasant methods were used by the army to try to force Henry and other objectors into line. He endured and was at last assigned to the medical corps. "These experiences of testing and of later service in the camp," said Fast, "represented a critical, but also a maturing, period in my life."

CPS as a theme from Russia
As war clouds gathered over Europe in 1939, the Western District chose H. A. Fast to be executive secretary of its peace committee. He was to counsel men in the Western District on how to respond to the draft likely to come. Soon Fast was on his way to Washington, D.C., to deal with the U.S. government and the Congress. The treatment of objectors to war in World War I had been a disaster for the peace churches as well as for the United States Army. Both wanted a better way, but the peace churches had to take the lead. Government was too busy getting ready for war to find a creative way of dealing with objectors.

Henry Fast had a clue. He had just visited Mennonites in Canada and South America who had recently come from Russia. They told of alternative service during World War I. Mennonite men in Russia did forestry and medical service in nonmilitary units while Fast was doing medical service in the army.

Fast along with Quaker and Church of the Brethren delegates proposed a network of camps where objectors would do work of national importance in place of going to war. Under Civilian Public Service, camps would be run and financed by the churches. Thus, that trip to Idaho was an urgent one. The church had to show that it could adequately administer such camps.

No caliber safe for life of peace
In 1945, when World War II was almost over, Henry Fast went to South America to deal with another government. Mennonites in Paraguay were concerned about their pact with the nation. Paraguay had given them special privileges: land for settlements and exemption from military service. They wanted to be sure that the war had not eroded their rights.

In east Paraguay, Fast found something amiss. Mennonites made long trips by horse and wagon to the river port to market their crops. As they passed through Paraguayan settlements along the way where they were exposed to robbers, they had begun to carry guns.

"The only reason we're safe," said one farmer, "is that they know we have guns."

That was a challenge Fast couldn't let pass. He argued the issue with the colony council. They didn't want to carry guns, they said, but they saw no other way. They were safe from abuse by the Paraguayans only if they carried guns. A gun less than 38 caliber was not good enough.

"That's the reasoning of the world," said Fast. "As followers of Christ, we have learned another way." How inconsistent it was to apply for special rights as nonresistant Christians when everyday practice belied their claim. He said that Mennonite Central Committee could not approach the Paraguayan Government with clear conscience until this matter was cleared up. "How could we," he asked, "when colony leaders show their lack of faith in the way of love and the protection of God?"

They got the point.

Rebuke for the brainy scholar
As director of MCC's aid program in Europe in 1951, Fast worked with a team of project leaders. One young man, fluent in French and German, worked with the French Mennonites. Though brilliant in history and theology, he wasn't doing well in his relations with his co-workers and was in trouble with European church leaders.

Orie O. Miller, MCC's executive secretary, and Harold S. Bender, historian and MCC board member, came to Basel to review program with Fast and his team. In the meeting, the young worker attacked his elders for what he saw as errors in strategy. Bender didn't say a word. He had great respect for a brilliant mind and wouldn't contradict genius, especially one with a sharp tongue.

But when no one else would reply to the challenge, Fast spoke up. Responsible for work in Europe, he had to mend fences which this worker had left in disrepair. As Fast had once taken on the burly farmer in Idaho, he dared to rebuke the brainy scholar in Basel.

Standing for Jesus in his own time
At one time, he responded less boldly. Revivalism came to Mountain Lake, Minnesota, during his early teens. Henry attended the revival meetings faithfully and listened carefully. In their zeal for converts, the traveling preachers exerted heavy personal pressure.

Yet Henry never responded to the altar calls. For this, he was made to feel guilty as one who resisted the wooing of the Holy Spirit. Indeed, he did want to obey the call of God. From earliest childhood, he had responded to Jesus and he always wanted to follow—accepting him as Savior and Lord. But he did not want to be pressured into taking that step. He wanted it to be a free and glad declaration of his own commitment.

And later, at nineteen, he did respond in a wholehearted way in a special act of dedication at the close of his first year of study at Bethel College.

Plea for unity from a Dutch uncle
While in South America in 1939, Henry visited the new Mennonite colonies in Brazil. The refugees from Russia were poor. They had settled in the hills along the Kraul River. It was a backbreaking, spirit-breaking task to clear the land. They had to deal with tough community issues when everybody was physically tired and mentally exhausted. At times, they said some sharp things to one another.

Just before Fast left Brazil, he was riding in a buggy with four or five of the Brazilian leaders. They were really pulling each other to pieces. One of the leading ministers was most bitter. Fast took it about as long as he could.

Then he began to talk like a Dutch uncle. "This is intolerable," he said, "that you, being leaders of your people, preachers of the Word and the gospel of forgiveness, should talk like this." He was scolding them. But they listened and quit arguing. It put a bit of a damper on the conflicts.

As a peacemaker, H. A. Fast was a pioneer. In meeting with conflict, he was always forthright. He was, after all, our pacifist with the square jaw.

RESOURCES:

Shelly, Maynard, 1981. "Henry A. Fast" *in* Cornelius J. Dyck, ed. *Something Meaningful for God: the Stories of Some Who Served with MCC.* Scottdale, PA: Herald Press. pp. 32-70.

Barry C. Bartel, 1983. "Henry A. Fast: a Man with a Purpose," unpublished paper with bibliography of writings by Fast [copy at Mennonite Library and Archives, North Newton, KS].

Mennonite Encyclopedia Vol. V. 1956. Scottdale, PA: Mennonite Publishing House, p. 295.

Jacob G. Ewert
Credit: Mennonite Library & Archives

A One Man Relief Agency

JACOB G. EWERT, 1874-1923

by Bertha Fast Harder

In 1882 an eight-year old boy named Jacob Ewert accompanied his parents as they moved from their home near Warsaw, Poland, to the United States of America. They settled in the new rural town of Hillsboro, Kansas. The people of Hillsboro came to know Jacob as a very bright boy; it was said that he finished the local public school's course of study by the age of 14. Family poverty prevented him from pursuing a well-rounded education, but he managed to earn a state teaching certificate and began to teach school while still in his teens. His father worked as the custodian for the First Mennonite Church of Hillsboro, of which he and Jacob were charter members.

In 1895 Jacob enrolled at Bethel College but was able to study only intermittently. He earned his way through college by tutoring and other types of work, and his bright intellect and capabilities now became apparent in the wider Mennonite community. Originally Bethel College had plans for a commercial department, but lack of funds made that prohibitive. Nevertheless, strong interest of other students prompted Jacob Ewert, a second-year student, to organize and teach a class in Stenography. He was also a member of the first Botany class at Bethel, a class reported to have been requested by the four or five students enrolled. Jacob, evidently inspired by the class subject, began in the spring and summer of 1896, to collect and press flowers and plants gathered on the prairie, the roadsides, and in the gardens of the community. He gave 379 sheets of this catalogued collection to the Bethel College Herbarium in the Science Department.

Just when his keen intellect and unusual inventiveness were beginning to find expression, something happened to this young man. Jacob Ewert was attacked by a rheumatoid arthritis that gradually caused nearly total paralysis. Physicians could not help him, and he was soon bedridden. For awhile he had partial use of his arms and hands; a picture of him during those early years shows an autoharp on his bed which he still managed to play. Little by little the paralysis worsened, and he was an invalid for the rest of his life, during the first two decades of this century.

His legs were cramped and all his joints were stiff. Even his jaw was immobile so that he had to be fed through a tube in his mouth. The only limb he could use was his right arm suspended in a sling and the thumb and one finger on his right hand.

After he was smitten with this crippling illness, Jacob made several decisions. First, he wrote an announcement in the Bethel College paper that all the students in his stenography class could continue the course by correspondence with him, free of charge. Second, and of greater significance for himself, he decided to continue his own studies in bed, for his paralysis had not affected his mind. On the contrary, as his body withered, his intellect became increasingly active. He was a master of English and German and went on now to become a scholar in Greek, Latin and Hebrew. Later he taught these languages to interested students from Tabor College as they came to visit him at his bedside. He also gained a fair reading and writing knowledge in several additional modern European languages including Russian.

He wanted and needed to find new ways of expressing his radical ideas, to share his creative thinking. More and more he found that he could express himself through the medium of writing. Jacob had a typewriter placed within reach of his right hand. While his arm hung in a sling, he could use his thumb and finger very laboriously to produce line after line of writing. He was assisted in this by his faithful brother, David. The two brothers often worked from early morning until late into the night; no one ever heard complaints from either man. Indeed, when others entered the room, they experienced good humor and cheer, as Jacob pecked away at the typewriter with David sitting near at hand. They saw a small string attached to the typewriter cylinder, and they observed with curiosity as David pulled it to return the carriage at the end of each line. When the page was full, David would carefully insert a clean sheet of paper.

As part of the process of making sense of his illness and pain, he wrote a 75-page booklet entitled *Der Gute Kampf, Eine Allegorie* (The Good Struggle, An Allegory). In all seriousness he asked the question, "Should a Christian be sick?" Someone had come to him and said, "Well, Brother Ewert, you are still sick! Get up! A child of God should not be lying down sick! Since I am in the state of sanctification, I have never been sick." Ewert replied, "Then I would rather identify with the Lord Jesus, who also became weary. My sickness is only an increased weariness."

Jacob wrote continually and with an open mind on all kinds of subjects and social concerns. On behalf of various causes, he wrote hundreds of letters and many articles for journals and papers. He took an active interest in the prohibition movement, and was elected secretary of the Kansas chapter. He was so much in sympathy with the socialistic views of the time that he wrote a booklet entitled, *Christentum und Sozialismus* (Christianity and Socialism), which went through several editions and printings. He was critical of societies and governments that favored the classes who were landed and rich; he argued that to be true to the teachings of Jesus, Christians should always be advocates for the poor.

Jacob found an advocate of his own in the person of Dr. Jacob Entz, a Hillsboro physician and publisher of a newspaper called *Das Freie Presse* (the Free Press), which later evolved into *The Hillsboro Journal*. At two stages in the development of these papers, Entz hired Ewert as his editor. This gave him another medium for his writing. As he wrote in an editorial, Jacob saw this position as "another way to fulfill the work that God had set for him as an invalid."

In his editorials Jacob did not hesitate to confront certain leaders in the community when he felt they were on the wrong track. Once, after confronting a local Mennonite land agent for questionable dealings, he was called a "sick editor." This prompted another editorial in which Jacob wrote as follows:

Even though "sick Ewert" is the editor of this newspaper, it is his endeavor to see that nothing sickly gets into the paper. He will always endeavor to have a sound eye and sense for human conditions and fortunes so that his horizons are not limited by the four walls of his sick room. Yet, now that he lives in his new bed with wheels on which he can easily get out into the free air, his contact with the outside world is not limited to the telephone alone, but he can also get out onto God's fertile land and into God's beautiful nature. Although he is not as free as other humans to travel into the wide world, yet he can see in the blue sky above the clouds moving along and send his thoughts on distant travels into the highs and the lows of the human heart.

As an ardent pacifist during World War I, Jacob served as counselor to many young men facing the draft. When the Mennonite conscientious objectors were being imprisoned at Camp Funston during World War I, J. G. Ewert defended them in the public press against the slanders and lies published about them in *The Kansas City Star* and *The Star*. To provide needed literature on pacifism, he translated the correspondence between the Russian writer Leo Tolstoy and the American pacifist Adin Ballou, through which Tolstoy embraced a radically pacifist position.

During all these years Jacob continued to read articles and books in many languages. It was his good fortune to have friends who subsidized his purchase of books in his fields of interest. When finished with the books, he donated them to the Bethel College Library at a time when that library was much in need of more books. In the last year of his life, 205 volumes in 12 different languages were donated by J. G. Ewert.

At the end of World War I, Ewert's greatest contribution came to pass. Russian postwar years were followed by the Communist Revolution, the War fought so near to the Mennonite villages in the Ukraine, bringing the terrorism of violent anarchist gangs, and the terrible famine and starvation of 1922-23. Always well informed on national and international issues, he was one of the first leaders at home to become aware of the dreadful needs in eastern Europe. He wrote articles for the various Mennonite papers calling attention to the need for aid from America. He began to write about more specific ways whereby American Mennonites could help. He communicated with various relief organizations—the American Red Cross, the American Friends Service Committee and Near East Relief. By helping his readers to become better informed, he inspired greater willingness to contribute funds for this worthy cause.

Meanwhile the new American Mennonite Relief Organization had been formed with Jacob Ewert having a role in opening the door to direct Mennonite relief work in the Ukraine, where our people were starving. After repeated unsuccessful attempts to get official permission to bring food relief into the Ukraine, our relief director, Alvin J. Miller, in desperation went to the Russian Foreign Office in Moscow. After many days of waiting and talking with lower echelon officials, he was finally able to see the head of the Anglo-American section of the Foreign Office, who had already become informed about the American Mennonite mission through a letter received from a Mr. J. G. Ewert of Hillsboro, Kansas, and brought to Moscow by a member of the Soviet Mission in the United States and presumably written in the Russian language.

In addition to permission to bring in shiploads of direct aid, arrangements were made for continuing family to family aid in the form of ten dollar food drafts. It was the filling out of the applications for food drafts that gave Jacob his last and greatest service opportunity. A knowledge of both English and Russian was required to fill out a food draft application, and hundreds of American Mennonites sent their ten dollar bills to Jacob Ewert, Hillsboro, Kansas, with instructions to send a food draft to Russia, often to a specific family and sometimes to wherever needed most. As an early MCC historian described it:

> The very modest home of this invalid with his brother and a very aged mother became the headquarters of thousands of such as wished to take advantage of the food-draft method of sending food to friends and relatives in Russia.... When

requests from the needy in Europe began to come in, a veritable deluge of food-draft applications poured forth from Bro. Ewert's home.

Great sums of money were entrusted to Jacob to help feed the hungry abroad. For months he and David worked on this from early morning until late at night. Records show that when the food-draft program came to an end on March 15, 1923, Jacob Ewert had processed applications totalling $89,000. With his last deposit of money at the First National Bank of Hillsboro, he added the following words to the deposit slip: "I have written the last food draft application. MY WORK IS DONE."

That night he became ill with influenza. Jacob Ewert grew rapidly weaker, and on the next day, March 16th, he died. As one writer put it, "The heroic soul in a wrecked body took flight."

RESOURCES:

Hiebert, P.C. 1929. The Contributions of J. G. Ewert. pp. 287-292. *In*: P.C. Hiebert and Orie O. Miller. *Feeding the Hungry: Russia Famine 1919-1925*. Scottdale, PA: Mennonite Central Committee.

Neff, Christian and J.W. Nickel. 1956. Jacob G. Ewert. pp. 273-274. *In*: *The Mennonite Encyclopedia, Vol. II*. Scottdale, PA: Mennonite Publishing House.

Wedel, Peter J. 1954. *In* Edmund G. Kaufman, ed. *The Story of Bethel College*. pp. 103, 122. North Newton, KS: Bethel College.

Wiebe, Raymond F. 1985. *The City on the Prairies*. Hillsboro, KS: Multi-Business Press, Inc., pp. 124-125, 133-134.

Sister Frieda Kaufman
Credit: Mennonite Library & Archives

The First Deaconess

SISTER FRIEDA KAUFMAN, 1883-1944

by Bertha Fast Harder

Well over a hundred years ago in Haagen Baden, Germany, in the year 1883, a little girl was born to Johannes and Marie Egle Kaufman. They named their baby daughter Frieda Marie. Their home was located in the Wiesen wooded valley, where during the time of winter and Christmas, the hills and woods of evergreen were covered with sparkling white snow.

As a little girl, Frieda loved Christmas more than any other time of the year. She helped her mother make cookies in exquisite forms of flowers, birds, animals and Christians designs. The best were saved to hang on the Christmas tree. Father always found a beautiful evergreen in the wooded hills for their Christmas tree. It was set up in the "best" room of the house— the parlor. On December 24th, Mother spent much of the day in the parlor behind locked doors, decorating the Christmas tree and getting everything ready for the Christmas Eve celebration. Frieda and her sisters were all dressed in their Sunday best, sitting and waiting—waiting for a special sound, the tinkling of a bell. Frieda could hardly wait! And then it happened!

The door of the parlor slowly opened wide, and there it was, the tall Christmas tree, ablaze with light, the light of countless candles flickering—a splendid sight to behold.

But Frieda and her sisters did not rush in. They knew better. They all entered the room quietly, because there was Father, standing beside the Christmas tree with the Bible in his hand. He read the story of Jesus' birth in an almost holy voice, and said a prayer.

Mother led the singing of Christmas carols in a clear, sweet voice. There was a nativity scene under the tree. Now the children could come close to the tree and admire the colorful decorations. Frieda loved the beautiful angel hanging on the tree best of all. It was made out of pink wax with widespread wings of gauze that looked like spun glass.

Then there were presents for everyone, for parents first. On a table were plates for each one, filled with nuts, cookies, sweets, a chocolate bar, an orange. What a glorious time was Christmas.

When Frieda was seven years old the family lived in a Roman Catholic community. She spent much time in the home of a group of nuns who lived across the street from the Kaufman family. Frieda came to be a friend of the nuns, and they were very kind to her. They gave her the much coveted privilege of helping with the small kindergarten children in their Home. One day Frieda decided, "Someday when I grow up, I want to be like a nun, a 'Sister.'"

When Frieda was nine years old the family decided to leave Europe and move to the United States. They settled in Halstead, Kansas. When December came to Kansas the first year, Father tried to buy a Christmas tree, but no one had any evergreens to spare. There were none for sale. "Oh Father, what will we do without a Christmas tree?" cried Frieda.

Father found a way. He took a heavy, tall stick, drilled holes into it, and put branches from a cedar tree given to him by a neighbor, into the holes. Frieda had her tree.

Mother found the box marked "Christmas tree decorations" and they began to unpack each ornament carefully. Frieda was eagerly waiting for her favorite tree decoration—the beautiful pink wax angel with the white gauze wings. And then she saw it! All that was left of the little angel was a pink mass of wax. It had melted in the hot Kansas summer! Even so, they had a joyful family Christmas.

Sadly, about two years later, Frieda's mother died. This shattered the family. The much-older sisters soon married and moved away. At the age of 16 years, Frieda was asked by her father to work for an older woman as a temporary housekeeper. This woman had a stroke and young Frieda took on the role of being her nurse as well, a job she loved to do—a job that fit in with her early dream of becoming a deaconess. (This was a term other Protestant churches in Europe were using in nursing and service for women.)

It was by chance that David Goerz heard of young Frieda Kaufman's interest in nursing and becoming a deaconess. He invited her to come and see him. Earlier, David Goerz had already expressed his dream regarding deaconess work in the conference, the larger church. He had read a paper before the General Conference Mennonite Church in 1890 advocating that deaconess service could become a part of Home Missions.

By 1900 Frieda Kaufman, then 17, offered herself to David Goerz as a candidate for the deaconess cause. He suggested that she enroll at the Bethel College Academy and study there until she would be old enough to enter deaconess training. This advice she followed.

The next important and complicated step for Frieda was to enroll at the Interdenominational Deaconess Hospital in Cincinnati, a place of training carefully searched out by David Goerz, and one that Frieda had approved prior to her entrance there. She completed the regular two-year course of instruction as arranged by Bethel College.

Frieda still needed and wanted experience in nursing. After returning to the Newton community, she offered her services as a private nurse, but few people were willing to pay for this. Frieda waited for calls that never seemed to come. Gradually the community came to accept and trust her nursing skills. It was a long, often lonely, and difficult struggle for Frieda.

One Christmas Eve she was at a distant farm home, taking care of a very sick woman. The husband had become ill as well, and since Frieda could not take adequate care of both, he had been taken to the hospital, leaving Frieda alone at this farm home on a bitterly cold Christmas Eve. During the evening the sick woman fell asleep. Frieda put on her warm, outdoor clothing and stepped outside to get some fresh air. The dark countryside was covered with snow. No lighted windows could be seen anywhere. But, oh, what a beautiful sky; so many stars and so brilliant. As

Frieda stood there she thought of that first Christmas night when Jesus Christ was born. It could not have been more beautiful.

She went back into the little house and saw that the woman was still fast asleep. Frieda thought of something else she wanted to do on this Christmas Eve. She lighted a kerosene lantern and walked out to the barn. There were the cows and horses, fast asleep, breathing heavily.

The animals wakened a bit, drowsily looking at the lighted lantern. All was so peaceful there in the barn. Frieda felt as if she were in the presence of that Holy Night. That night she never forgot.

During all this time Frieda was waiting for her dream to be a deaconess realized. Finally the Bethel Deaconess Home and Hospital was dedicated on June 11, 1908, and Frieda was one of the first three deaconesses to be ordained and to move into the new hospital.

The now "Sister Frieda" became the Sister-in-Charge. This brought a myriad of very responsible assignments. She took on the role of Sister Superior of the now-formed Sisterhood. She was Director of Religious Life, which meant she was responsible for the religious life of the Sisters, the student nurses, the patients, and all personnel housed on the premises. Her duties included weekly prayer meetings and Bible classes, Sunday morning services, times of daily devotions for the Sisters, student nurses and for the patients. More than that, she was also Director of Public Relations. She supervised the sewing room and the purchase of all dry goods.

In time she was given many other administrative tasks, even that of Hospital Administrator! Sister Frieda had a strong personality. Some may have thought she became a bit authoritarian at times. However, they would agree that she also had the fine quality of great sensitivity.

Sister Frieda loved celebrations and made them a part of the life of the Sisterhood, which was really like a family. The time of Christmas was the greatest of all times for celebration according to Sister Frieda. Each year a big Christmas tree was placed behind locked doors in the dining room of the hospital. Secretly, Sister

Frieda trimmed the tree with white candles and sometimes red apples. Boxes and packages that came in the mail for anyone under her charge were intercepted and put in that locked dining room to be opened on Christmas Eve. Meanwhile decorations and candles graced the whole hospital and Deaconess Home. The Sisters and student nurses practiced Christmas cantatas. There was caroling in the halls and in the streets of Newton. Groups of nurses and others went to visit prisoners in jail.

Finally, on Christmas Eve, the door to the dining room was opened by Sister Frieda at her bidding. There stood the tall Christmas tree, resplendent with the flickering lights of real candles. This highest time of celebration was open for all, the Sisters, nurses, student nurses, hospital staff, relatives, friends, children. Surely this was Sister Frieda's highest moment of realized joy.

As fulfilling as all these ministries were for her, Sister Frieda had other dreams. An unmet need of older persons in the community could find a solution in the establishing of a Home for the Aged. She realized that she had to educate the public for this need. She helped to organize a fund-raising campaign. She helped in drawing the plans. The Bethel Home for the Aged became a model for its time.

Sister Frieda was deeply involved in the First Mennonite Church in Newton. She was a Sunday school teacher. She was instrumental in their placing stained glass windows in the sanctuary and influenced the choice of the color of the bricks.

Sister Frieda was a literary person. She read widely, and wrote profusely in the publication *In the Service of the King*. The hymn, "What Mercy and Divine Compassion" (#68 in the *Mennonite Hymnal*) was translated by her from the German language.

Sister Frieda had a great appreciation for Bethel College. The college had made the deaconess cause a part of its program as early as 1901. She felt that Bethel had a significant role to play, not only in education, but as a symbol of culture and in promoting religious life in the Newton community and beyond.

In 1937 she was made a member of the Bethel College faculty in the division of the practical arts. For several years she served on the Advisory Council, which was an effort to link the college more closely with geographically distant Mennonite communities in support of the college.

In a surprising and crowning recognition of her services, Bethel College honored Sister Frieda by granting her an honorary Doctor of Humane Letters degree in 1942. The Citation read to Bethel College President E. G. Kaufman was as follows in part:

> Sister Frieda, more than any other, has been instrumental in establishing the Deaconess cause in the Mennonite Church of North America. Women who have known her as a teacher and counsellor have caught a vision that has enabled them to go to France, to Belgium, to India, to China, to Africa, to the plateaus of Tibet in order to carry, through the medium of nursing, the torch of God's redemptive love.
>
> Mr. President, in recognition of these unique and distinguished services and upon recommendation of the faculty, and the unanimous vote of the Board of Directors, we herewith present Sister Frieda Marie Kaufman for the honorary degree of the Doctor of Humane Letters.

There is a report that tells of someone finding Sister Frieda on the day after receiving the great honor, on her hands and knees scrubbing the floor of a hospital room. She is supposed to have explained her action by saying she was scrubbing the floor, "so that I may not become proud."

Sister Frieda died on August 7, 1944, shortly after a heart attack, but her life and work were not forgotten years later. A memorial chapel was built and dedicated in honor of all the deaconesses. The chapel was named Sister Frieda Memorial Chapel. It has been used for countless religious functions during all these years.

Now that chapel has become the house of meeting for the New Creation Fellowship. It is alive today. It is alive with the voices of women, men, and children singing and praying, speaking, studying, in fellowship and worship—a beautiful and fitting memorial for Sister Frieda Marie Kaufman.

RESOURCES:

Bartel, Marilyn. 1966. Sister Frieda Marie Kaufman, Builder of Institutions and Lives. Student paper. Bethel College. North Newton, Kansas.

Deaconess. *Mennonite Encyclopedia. Vol. II.* 1956. Scottdale, PA: Mennonite Publishing House. p. 24.

Kaufman, Edmund G. 1973. *General Conference Mennonite Pioneers.* North Newton, KS: Bethel College.

Kaufman, Sister Frieda Marie. *Christmas Reverie.* [available in Mennonite Historical Library].

Sister Frieda Kaufman. *Mennonite Encyclopedia. Vol. III.* p. 158.

Unrau, Ruth. 1986. Sister Frieda. *Encircled.* pp. 73-81.

John Schrag
Credit: Loris A. Habegger

"Creek John" Won't Buy

JOHN SCHRAG

by James C. Juhnke

John Schrag was a prosperous Mennonite farmer who lived in Alta township, Harvey County, Kansas. He was a member of the Hopefield Mennonite Church. To distinguish him from other men in the community who were also named John Schrag, people called him "Creek John." Actually, because everyone in the congregation spoke German early in this century, "Creek John" was called "*Krickehannes*." Near his farmstead two creeks flowed into the Little Arkansas river. That was as good an excuse for a nickname as anything.

When America went to war against Germany in 1917, Creek John got into trouble. There were three problems. First, the war was good for his bank account. The price of wheat more than doubled. Second, he spoke the German language. American citizens suspected any German-speakers of sympathizing with their war enemy. Third, he was a nonresistant Christian. He believed it was wrong to fight in war, or to pay for other people to do the killing.

The United States government decided to pay for the war in 1917 with voluntary contributions from citizens. All over the country they set up local committees to conduct War Bond Drives. People were so enthusiastic about this war that they were willing to pay for it voluntarily. They invested in bonds which they would be able to cash in after the war for a small rate of interest. Everybody was supposed to contribute according to their ability to pay.

When the war bond committee came from the town of Burrton to collect from Creek John, they expected a substantial contribution. They reminded him about his big wheat fields and the rising price of wheat. But Schrag refused to buy war bonds. He was a Mennonite, he said, and Mennonites did not contribute to war.

In fact, some Mennonites did buy war bonds. They argued that the bonds were a kind of tax, because there was so much official pressure to pay. In the Bible, Jesus said to pay taxes.

Schrag said the war bonds were not a tax. He refused to pay, even when the committee came back several times, and was put on their blacklist.

On November 11, 1918, the day the First World War ended, the citizens of Burrton called a holiday and held a big victory celebration. Some fellows set up a casket with a sign that the Kaiser, the leader of the defeated German nation was inside. There was a dead skunk in the casket.

The Burrton war bond committee decided this would be a good time to get Creek John to finally buy some war bonds. They took five carloads of men eleven miles out to the Schrag farm to get the Mennonite farmer to come to town for the celebration. Creek John had no choice but to come along. Back in Burrton they told him they would give him one more chance. He had to buy bonds now or face the consequences. He refused once again.

They tried to get Schrag to carry an American flag and lead a parade through town. Someone put a flag to his hand, but he did not take hold of it and it fell to the ground. Someone in the milling crowd shouted, "He stepped on the American flag!" The crowd turned into an uncontrollable mob.

They started pushing and beating Creek John. Someone got a bucket of yellow paint. They poured it over him, and rubbed it into his scalp and beard. The Burrton *Graphic* newspaper account later said he looked like "a big cheese or yellow squash or pumpkin after the autumnal ripening."

They took Creek John over to the city jail, a little calaboose which stood to the side of Main Street. Someone brought a rope and said that instead of putting him in jail they should hang him to a tree. They would have hanged Creek John had not Tom Roberts stepped in.

Tom Roberts was the head of the Burrton Anti-Horse-Thief Association, a force for law and order. Roberts pulled out his gun, got Schrag into the jail, and said, "We are Americans. This man is going to get a fair trial. If he is guilty, he will be punished. You won't take him out of this jail except over my dead body."

Some of the frustrated mob members made other plans. They decided to come back that night under cover of darkness when the jail would not be heavily guarded. They could then overcome the guards and hang Creek John after all.

When they came back that night, Creek John was gone. Someone had called the Harvey County Sheriff who came out and took him to the county jail in Newton for safekeeping. The sheriff helped him get cleaned and released him the next day. But it still wasn't clear that he was out of danger. The *Hutchinson News* of November 16, 1918, reported, "a petition is being circulated to have him (Schrag) deported to Germany, his native land. This country is fast becoming an unhealthy place for 'slackers' of any kind."

The Burrton citizens decided to bring Creek John to court on charges of violating the Espionage Act, which made it crime to show disrespect to the American flag. They compiled fifty typewritten pages of evidence for the court. Creek John hired a Jewish lawyer from Wichita to defend him.

In a decision handed down on December 24, 1918, the judge ruled that Creek John was not guilty. The Espionage Act did not require anyone to salute the flag. The evidence that Creek John had slandered the flag was not convincing. Everything he had said that day was in German. None of his accusers could speak or understand German. In reporting the judge's decision, the Newton *Evening Kansan-Republican* of December 27 said the case "should certainly make plain to any thinking person the viciousness that exists in the encouragement of the German language as a means of communication in America.... The melting pot cannot exercise its proper functions when such things are allowed."

Creek John's lawyer told him to take his persecutors to court. There was no doubt that they had violated his rights as a citizen.

But Creek John declined to sue. That would have gone against Mennonite nonresistant principles.

There is an important footnote to the story of Creek John's persecution in Burrton, Kansas, on November 11, 1918. One member of the mob was Charles Gordon, a young dairy farmer who had come into town for the celebration. Mr. Gordon couldn't get out of his mind what he had seen and done. Years later he told how Creek John had responded to his persecutors:

> I don't know how many people walked right up to him and spit in his face and he never said a word. And he just looked up all the time we was doing that. Possibly praying, I don't know. But there was some kind of a glow come over his face and he just looked like Christ.... Enemies smite you on one cheek, turn the other. And brother, he did it. He just kept doing it. They'd slug him on the one side of the face and he'd turn his cheeks on the other. He exemplified the life of Christ more than any man I ever saw in my life.

Because of the witness of Creek John, Charles Gordon became a nonresistant Christian.

RESOURCES:

Juhnke, James C. "John Schrag Espionage Case," *Mennonite Life*, July 1967, pp. 121-122.

Transcript of tape-recorded interview with Charles Gordon. Mennonite Library and Archives at Bethel College. Part of the transcript was published in *Mennonite Life*, September 1975, pp. 20-21.

Lehn, Cornelia, 1980. "To Pay or Not to Pay," *Peace Be With You*. Newton, KS: Faith and Life Press. p. 83.

Peter P. Wedel
Credit: Mennonite Library & Archives

When Dreams Come True

PETER P. WEDEL

by David C. Wedel

When he was still a small boy they called him Pete. His real name was Peter. Sometimes he was called Peter P. Wedel. Most of the time he was called P. P. Wedel. We may not be able to tell when Peter had a dream about becoming a minister. We know that even before he could understand a sermon he would see his uncle, John C. Goering, stand in the pulpit in the church, saying something very important. When he began to understand some things in the sermon, he knew he wanted to stand in the pulpit to do what Uncle John was doing. When he was growing up every time he was asked what he wanted to be, he would say, "I want to be a preacher."

He did not know when his dream would come true. He thought it would happen some day a long time away, so he spent many days being a busy helpful boy. He played like all other sons of pioneer settlers living on the Kansas prairie. At times he would get to go along to the town of Moundridge which was built on land owned by his grandfather, Johannes Wedel. Sometimes he had to stay at home and work because in those days all children of pioneer families had to help with the farm work.

Peter's parents were earnest Christians who taught their children that we have a Savior, Jesus Christ. They took him to Sunday School and like every child, he stayed in church for the worship hour. Just where Peter sat in the church we do not know, but he learned to listen and learned the hymns that were sung in the church services.

When he was sixteen years of age he had an experience which made a deep impression on him. In a simple but beautiful service he was baptized and dedicated his life to Jesus Christ. From that day on he resolved to do whatever God wanted him to do. He was saying what Isaiah once said, "Here am I Lord, send me." He never forgot what he had promised God on that day. He hoped God would say, "I want you to be a preacher." The more he thought of this, the more he wanted to preach, but he thought that day was still far away. He attended school, worked, and enjoyed the love of his family in the useful activities of farm life. He was nearly sixteen when he graduated from Moundridge Junior High School. It was a momentous occasion because this was the first class to graduate from this school.

Rather suddenly his hopes began to take form. Rev. John C. Goering, Uncle John as he was known by the family, asked the church to provide a helper. The church agreed that someone should be found to help Uncle John. This was not too difficult for the church to do. It was the custom that helpers would be found within the membership of the church. An election was held and the two candidates who received the highest number of votes were chosen by lot. The names of the two were placed in the Bible and the candidates drew a slip of paper which would tell who was chosen to be a minister.

Would this be the time when Peter's hopes would be fulfilled? He did not think so even though Uncle John had asked him, "Pete, would you not want to be a minister of the gospel?" Peter thought that some day his name would be on that slip of paper in the Bible—but not now. To his surprise the church gave him enough votes to be one of the candidates for the drawing of the lot. Just what his thoughts were or what Peter had prayed before the day of the drawing of the lot we do not know, but the moment came to draw the lot out of the Bible. Peter could hardly read the words on the slip of paper, *"Der Herr hat Dich berufen."* (The Lord has chosen you.)

What should Peter do now? He was not ready to assume such a responsibility. He asked whether he might be an apprentice to "Uncle John" to discover whether he wanted to be ordained; he did not want to be ordained immediately. Besides he would need more education. He was only nineteen years of age. Would the congregation really accept him as an assistant minister?

In January 1904, Peter enrolled at Bethel College. He graduated in the spring of 1906, having pursued the Evangelistic Course. During this time he also began to preach whenever Uncle John wanted him to. He gave his first sermon on April 4, 1904. One year later, on July 1, 1905, he was ordained. Twelve years later he was ordained as Elder, and took over the responsibilities as pastor of the First Church of Christian, Moundridge, Kansas. He preached from this same pulpit for 46 years, retiring from the position July 1, 1968.

P. P. Wedel, as he was known in church and conference circles, was a serious student. Seven years after he preached his first sermon, he moved his family to the Bethel College campus for more education, but he continued to preach. Every Sunday he would trot his horses the eighteen miles to the church, missing only two Sundays during the two years he attended Bethel College. Several times the snow was so deep that his ponies could not get through the snowdrifts, so he walked the railroad tracks to get to his church. Later the Wedels built a house near the church, where they lived until they moved to a retirement home in 1966.

Peter did his work well and soon became deeply involved in the work of the Western District Conference and the General Conference of the Mennonite Church. In the Western District he served on the Education Committee, the Home Missions Committee, as vice-president and president, and on the Board of Trustees. In the General Conference he served as vice president, as president of the Board of Foreign Missions, and on the Board of Directors of Bethel College. He was often asked to speak, both in the United States and in Canada.

How often did P. P. Wedel preach? He had 73 series of evangelistic meetings in different parts of the country. He preached more than 4,000 sermons, conducted 333 funerals, married 155 couples, baptized 310 persons, ordained nine ministers and 18 missionaries, and dedicated four churches.

Because of his faithful services and tireless leadership, Bethel College honored him by conferring the degree of Doctor of Divinity in 1944.

P. P. Wedel's ministry covered a time of progress and of confusion. World War I and II took place during his service. He began his ministry when the German language was the language of the church. On Sunday, August 28, 1918, Rev. Wedel found a slip of paper on each door of the church which read, "Notice, no more German services will be allowed at this church." After much thought Rev. Wedel decided to preach in German in spite of this warning. After German was no longer the official language of the church, he became a proficient preacher in the English language. His wisdom and counsel were sought by many who found themselves in various life situations.

After his retirement as minister, he asked for the privilege of being the janitor of his church.

He passed away in November of 1973.

Samuel S. Haury
Credit: Mennonite Library & Archives

Samuel Haury and Running Buffalo

SAMUEL S. HAURY

by James C. Juhnke

In November 1876 in Halstead, Kansas, Samuel S. Haury reported to the delegates at the Western District Conference about his quest for a mission field. He had just returned from a wagon trip to Indian Territory (now Oklahoma). On his trip he heard that some Plains Indians had the custom of killing a horse when an important person died, so he can be carried to the happy hunting grounds and have a horse for use there. Horses were important to the Indians.

Eight years later, Haury and his wife, Susie, were missionaries among the Cheyenne people at Cantonment. Their work was difficult. They found themselves in a conflict between persecuted Native Americans and land-hungry whites. In early May of 1884, a conflict between cowboys and Indians almost exploded into warfare—right on the Mennonite mission station. Haury had to be the peacemaker. The battle was over some horses.

Here is how it happened.

One Sunday morning three cowboys, led by a man named E. M. Horton, were driving a herd of 400 ponies northward through Indian Territory toward Kansas. They needed to cross the North Canadian river. Apparently their normal route was impassable because of heavy rains, so they took an alternative route which was about five miles east of the Mennonite Mission Station at Cantonment. This route also happened to run across Indian reservation land belonging to a Cheyenne Dog Soldier named Running Buffalo.

When the cowboys with their horses arrived, Running Buffalo stopped them and demanded the payment of two horses for the right of passage. Horton refused to pay. The men argued furiously.

Suddenly their exchange of words turned into an exchange of gunfire. We don't know exactly how it happened. The cowboys said the Indians fired first. Perhaps Running Buffalo shot his rifle into the air; perhaps he shot into the herd of horses to scatter them. Whoever fired first, we do know who drew human blood. The cowboys shot and killed the Cheyenne Indian, Running Buffalo.

Soon other Indians arrived and threatened to overwhelm the three cowboys. The white men abandoned their ponies and fled on horseback to the nearest place of safety—the Mennonite mission station at Cantonment. That station had once been a military post, abandoned by the government and given to the Mennonites because the Indians had been "pacified." Now the cowboys found refuge in a small building in the middle of the mission station at the former telegraph office. They pointed their guns out, threatening to kill the Indians who surrounded the building at a distance.

Missionary Haury was teaching Sunday School in the main building when he heard all the ruckus outside. He was shocked to learn that the cowboys had killed Running Buffalo, a man he considered his friend. Indeed, they had shared a meal the previous Sunday. Haury quickly realized this to be a dangerous situation. The Cheyenne had enough men to overwhelm the three cowboys, though not without loss of life. But if the white men were killed, that would give an excuse for other whites to go on a rampage against the Indians. They stood right on the edge of a war between cowboys and Indians.

Haury sent someone to get the U.S. Cavalry from Fort Reno, 25 miles away. He started a process of mediation—going back and forth across no-mans-land to talk to each side and cool things down. He was the only person who was trusted by both sides. He tried to get the cowboys and Indians to meet and discuss a settlement face to face. At one point he thought he had both sides agreeing to disarm and meet half way; then the cowboys refused to come. It was a dangerous and frustrating effort, but in one thing Haury was successful. There was no more killing before the cavalry arrived to restore order.

Under the supervision of the U.S. Cavalry, an agreement was reached. In exchange for the life of their fellow tribesman, Running Buffalo, the Cheyenne would receive 200 ponies —half of the herd. In addition, the cowboys would be arrested and brought to trial for murder in the white man's court in Wichita, Kansas.

Several weeks later Haury traveled to Wichita to testify at the trial of Horton and the other two cowboys. He sympathized with the Cheyenne, but he could do nothing to prevent the course of the white man's justice. The cowboys insisted that Running Buffalo had fired first, and that they had only fired in self-defense. The judge accepted their testimony. He went on to rule that they were innocent, and therefore the agreement which gave 200 ponies to the Cheyenne was not valid. The Cheyenne had to return the ponies.

Mennonite mission work among the Cheyenne and Arapaho Indians was extremely difficult. Early in his ministry, Haury had written that he hoped to help overcome the decades of injustice that Native Americans had experienced at the hands of white people. How difficult it must have been for him to tell the Cheyenne that they had to return their ponies to the cowboys. What chance would the good news of the gospel have when it was mixed in with such awful news from the world? The new Mennonite church in Indian Territory grew very, very slowly.

Back in 1884 missionary Haury had to console himself with smaller achievements. After all, he did know that he had kept a war from breaking out between cowboys and Indians on a Mennonite mission station.

RESOURCES:

Haury, Samuel S. "*Bericht einer Untersuchungsreise* in Indian Territory," *Der Mennonitische Friedensbote,* Dec. 1, 1876, pp. 178-180.

Lehn, Cornelia. 1983. "Why Had He Failed," *I Heard Good News Today.* Newton, KS: Faith and Life Press, pp. 125-126.

[The first published account of the conflict between cowboys and Indians on the Mennonite mission station was in the *Christlicher Bundesbote,* June 1, 1884, p. 87.]

Jacob Reimer Duerksen
Credit: Mennonite Library & Archives

A Tin Box and a Bicycle

JACOB REIMER DUERKSEN

by Lois Duerksen Deckert

His tow head surfaced through the hole in the ice for the third time. Jacob's big brother, John, pulled him out of the icy water of the creek near their rural Hillsboro country school. Was that when Jacob Reimer Duerksen began to know that his life had a purpose?

Jacob Duerksen did not need unlimited equipment or high-tech inventions to do his work. He made do with simple things like a tin box, a bicycle, and a conviction that God had called him to preach, teach, and make disciples.

In the mid-1920s the General Conference Mission Board had money problems. Money to send missionaries overseas was often inadequate. There was none to send Jacob Duerksen and his wife, Christena Harder Duerksen, to India after they answered God's call to service. Jacob, known as J. R., had inherited some land from his father. He would not need that property if he went to India, he reasoned. So he sold it and gave the money to the Mission Board. This gift enabled J.R. and Christena to fulfill what they knew was God's destiny for them.

Entering British India put expectations on white people. They were expected to live in huge houses built to protect them from the blistering heat of summer. They were expected to hold top positions of leadership, they were expected to be waited on by uniformed servants, and the men were often expected to be great hunters. This was not J. R.'s style, even though he did once help shoot a leopard that was troubling a village. He was a man who would rather sit in a circle on the floor with his Indian colleagues than in a chair-level command position. He lived simply, not only because money was scarce, but because that was the way he chose to live. He could always find someone who needed his money more than he did. It meant that his family lived simply, too. Because J. R. was my dad, it meant that my siblings and I could not always have everything we wanted.

We did have cars. The first one I remember was a Model T Ford which was easily repaired with baling wire and lots of sweat. It needed cranking. The second was a Model A Ford donated for "the work" by a church in the U.S. We named this blue car Frieda. She served us well on the 95 mile trip to the railroad at least twice a year when we children went off to boarding school and when we came home for our three-month vacation. But most of the time Frieda sat idle because World War II fuels were severely rationed. J. R. preferred to ride his Hercules bicycle.

The evangelistic work to which J. R. joyfully and prayerfully gave his energy spanned a wide area around Jagdeeshpur in Central India. The rutted roads and narrow paths leading to the villages of Phuljar district went through jungles, across rivers, through muddy swamps and on the tops of the dikes around rice fields. J. R. would go out for a few days or weeks at a time to connect with remote churches and Indian evangelists. He came back with stories of his adventures, some humorous, some almost scary.

Sometimes I got to help him get ready for these village trips. I helped pack the tin box with toasted zwieback, roasted peanuts, a packet of tea and another of sugar and whatever other food fit in. This food provided breakfast. Dad usually ate the main meal of the day with his hosts or in other village homes.

One time an Indian evangelist said to Mother, "We thank God for Duerksen Sahib. We were in the home of new Christians. They wanted to serve us a meal. The rice was soggy and the vegetables tasteless. Duerksen Sahib ate his food as though it was a banquet, then thanked the host and hostess for the delicious meal. We Indians could hardly eat the food."

Besides the tin box of food, he carried a small bedroll with extra clothes, his tire patching kit, simple tools for bike repair, first aid supplies, his Bible and hymnbook, books for sale and books requested by the village pastors. The sale books were usually copies of the gospels. I also remember a songbook with a bright pink cover. All of these things were tied tightly onto the bicycle's rear carrier. Because village water was not sanitary, in fact teemed with bacteria detrimental to digestive tracts, Dad carried a large canteen of water.

When he was ready to go, his pant guard bunching his one pant leg tightly onto his ankle, we hugged him and gave him a long string of advice like "Don't fall." "Don't let a tiger get you." "Come home soon."

Every night that he was gone, after my bedtime story and prayers, I faced in the directions of the village to which he'd gone and blew him silver, gold, ruby, emerald, and diamond kisses. When he came home we welcomed him with hugs, and my brother Joe had the privilege of helping him get the bike cleaned up and ready for the next trip.

One day, when he'd planned a short trip, he asked me if I wanted to come along. A short trip for him was a 10 to 15-mile one, and usually just a day trip. I wriggled excitedly inside as I helped him tie a pillow onto the bar between the seat and the handlebars. This would be my sidesaddle seat. The back carrier would have been more comfortable but the tin box and other things were tied on there. In any case he didn't like us to ride on the carrier. One time my sister, Christine, sat on the carrier when she rode with him. Her heel caught in the spokes and was badly torn up. Ever since then J. R. was cautious about letting anyone ride on the carrier.

On the dusty, bumpy road we passed pedestrians and carts and cyclists. We exchanged friendly greetings with other travelers in the customary courtesy of the road. Women in their draped saris carried baskets of produce or other things on their heads. Men carried loaded baskets on a pole across their shoulders, the baskets bouncing rhythmically with each step. Cart drivers shouted at their slow-moving water buffaloes who pulled the heavy wooden-wheeled carts in a wood-on-wood-axle-squeaking line. Now and then a pair of flashy, matched, trotting bullocks with pointed horns and jingling bells passed everyone up. Their drivers swung whips, rubbed on the bullocks' spines or twisted their tails to maintain speed. We pedaled along on the road which was built up with steep sides. A footpath ran parallel below the raised road bed.

Over halfway to our destination it felt as if the cushions on the bar had disappeared. My dad stopped in a small village. He wanted to see if the shop keeper had a smaller bicycle for hire. I don't remember how old I was, but I had learned to ride a bicycle. While Dad talked to the man I decided to try riding down the village street a short way. I could barely reach the pedals when they were at the low point of their rotation. I took the bike to a low wall and from that vantage was able to straddle the bar. With a push I was off. "Don't go too far," Dad called.

Before I knew it I was past the last mud-walled house. The sides of the road became steep again. I wanted to turn around. The crowded road and steep sides allowed for no wide U-turns. My stomach felt tight, my legs felt rubbery, and I saw no low wall I could use as a stopping step. I could have let myself fall sideways, but somehow that had no appeal. I rode on, wobbling, but managing to keep my balance.

My dad couldn't rent another bike for me to ride. He said good-bye to the shopkeeper and looked down the road. He saw me in the distance and knew I was in trouble. He ran to catch up. The cart drivers coming toward him hollered from their perches, "She is getting very tired, Sahib." He ran on. I rode on.

This might have ended as a Phuljar marathon, but all at once the road dipped into a gully. The steep sides were gone and I saw an expanse of flat earth, enough for a wide and wobbly turn. By the time my Dad and I met, I was sobbing. He caught the handle bars and gently lifted me down. He should have scolded me, but he didn't.

We each had a drink of water from the canteen. We were tired and hot, but Dad had an appointment to meet. I crawled back on the bar in side-saddle position, and he sat on the seat. We were in our proper places again. We reached our destination in good Indian Standard time.

That was the last time I rode the bicycle bar to a village. I would have to wait for another trip with Dad until I was big enough to ride properly, turn decently, and stop on my own.

J. R. went on riding from village to village caring for those in his charge with his tin box on the back of his bicycle. He rode until a new assignment kept him classroom-bound in Janjgir.

Martha Richert Penner
Credit: Mennonite Library & Archives

Mamaji to Some, Aunty to Others

MARTHA RICHERT PENNER

by Lois Duerksen Deckert

She could hardly believe the good news she had just heard. Her best friend, Martha Richert, was going to marry Peter A. Penner. Agnes Harder Wiens was so excited she couldn't sleep.

Agnes and her husband, Peter J. Wiens, had gone to India after P. A. Penner's first wife, Elizabeth, died there. P. A. came back to the United States and during his furlough married Martha Richert, a deaconess and a member of the Alexanderwohl Mennonite Church.

The two friends, Agnes and Martha, had said good-bye to each other when they left nursing school in Cincinnati, Ohio. Now they would be close again. Perhaps if dancing had been permitted, Agnes would have danced for joy. And maybe on the other side of the seven seas, Martha felt the same kind of excitement added to the excitement of marriage and a new adventure.

Martha Richert Penner and her friend Agnes were as close as any sisters could be, even though they were not related by blood. During all their years in India their friendship remained strong. Agnes's children felt like beloved nieces and nephews in Martha's home. They claim that Martha always took their side when they were in trouble with their mother. Both Martha and Agnes lived in Newton, at Bethel Home for the Aged at the end of their lives.

Martha had no biological children but she had many children who called her Mamaji or Aunty. The missionary children called her Aunty Martha, but only Donald and Paul Isaac were real nephews. Don tells about a lesson in courtesy his mother tried to teach his little brother Paul.

My brother Paul, who lived only three and a half years, and I were fortunate that we had an uncle and aunt living within easy walking distance. Although Paul was three years younger than I was, he had a more impulsive nature.

One day Paul came home from Penners with sticky fingers. It was obvious he had eaten candy given him by Aunty Martha.

"Paul, did Aunt Martha give you some candy?" asked mother.

"Yes," said Paul, looking sheepish.

"Did you say thank you?"

"No, I didn't," answered Paul.

"Then we will go right back, and you can tell her that."

When they came to Aunt Martha's house mother said, "All right Paul, what do you say?"

"More *meetai* (candy)," replied Paul, who was sure of his Aunt Martha's generosity.

Aunt Martha's hospitality never wavered. Frieda Wiens Epp Krehbiel remembers the warm baths and clean sheets waiting in the guest room when they came to Champa after long trips or just on a visit from Mauhadhi where they lived. Travel was difficult and dusty, making warm baths and clean sheets much more important than they would be where travel was easy. She remembers the luxury foods that often appeared on the Penner table. For instance, instead of the more common white buffalo butter, Aunt Martha served imported yellow butter that came in tins. Her namesake, Martha Wiens Koehn, remembers Aunt Martha's lemon pies as the best ones she ever tasted.

The mischievous Wiens twins, Frieda and Martha, tested Aunt Martha's sense of humor one time when they were in Champa to celebrate her birthday. They slipped quietly to the bedroom and quickly short-shected Aunt Martha's bed. Then they waited in giggly expectation. They were rewarded the next morning with a chuckle and an eye twinkling recognition that it was all in fun.

Not only the missionary children remember Aunt Martha's generosity, good humor and love. A large group of girls called her Mamaji. These girls' parents had leprosy, and in those days children were taken away from parents with the disease. Aunt Martha was in charge of the untainted girls' boarding. Not only were the girls cared for—they also went to school, a rarity for village girls in those days.

Another group of girls found a home at the boarding, too. They were the babies either orphaned or abandoned. A girl was considered a liability, especially for a poor family who could not afford marriage for their daughter. Martha Wiens Koehn remembers how Aunt Martha cared for tiny babies in her home until they were strong enough to go into the boarding. The small crib in her bedroom and the constantly lit night light attested to the concern she had for the little ones.

When I learned to know her, she looked like a doting grandma. Her short, plump body, gray hair and kind smile gave her that appearance. As a child, whose own grandmas were far away, I was sure that Aunt Martha Penner looked exactly like grandmas were supposed to look.

Yet, at this grandma's house, I and all the other missionary children knew that certain courtesies must be maintained. It never felt proper to give way to rowdiness at Aunt Martha and Uncle P. A.'s house—I only put the leather hassock on its side for a good stomach roll over it one time. I found out immediately that children could play quietly with the toys provided, but the furniture stayed put.

Meals at the Penner house were elegant affairs. The adults sat at the big table, and we children sat at a little one. We were close enough to hear the conversation of the adults if we wanted to listen but far enough from the big table so that we could have our own conversation.

Chain (pronounced chaa-een), the cook, summoned guests to meals by playing a four-note tune on chimes which looked like a small xylophone. Sometimes we were allowed to play the chimes, too. Chain dressed in a white coat with wide, colored belt and wore a fancy turban when he served meals.

Aunt Martha liked to tell the story about the time she received a beautiful new tea cozy. The embroidered, thickly quilted tea cozy was about the size of a hat and fit snugly over the tea pot to keep it warm. One night when she planned dinner for guests she took out her new tea cozy. She told her cook that she wanted him to use this to serve tea. When the dinner ended and it was time for the tea, she rang the bell to summon the cook. She saw Chain coming from the kitchen and said to her guests, "You must not laugh when the tea is served." The guests had only a moment to wonder what she meant. In came the cook looking like a regal rajah with the tea cozy on his head.

Aunt Martha had some other stories she told on herself, stories that usually got us children giggling. Even before she fully learned Hindi she had to tell her servants what to do. One day she thought she asked her cook for a *chumuch* (spoon), but what she really asked for was a *chuma* (kiss). The cook was horrified. Men did not touch women, even their wives, in public—let alone kiss them. To kiss Mamaji Martha would be an unheard of breach of etiquette. Fortunately, in spite of her insistence, he knew better than to comply, and in the end they both figured out the problem. On another occasion she wanted some *chunna* (roasted chick peas) for a snack. She ordered *chenna* (dried cow dung cakes used for fuel). This time she got what she ordered. No matter, the iron cook stove could burn that as well as wood, even though the odor was slightly different and it made a smokier fire.

The last time I saw Aunt Martha she lived in the Bethel Home for the Aged. She was still a gracious hostess in her single room, concerned about all her grown-up children around the world and still wanting them to succeed and live the lives God intended for them.

Mary Thiessen Goering

German Schools

MARY THIESSEN GOERING

by Marlene Krehbiel

Education has always been an important part of the Mennonite community; it continued when the many Mennonite communities of Russia became the Mennonite communities of central Kansas. Schools were established within the first winter after their arrival. Because the mother tongue of the Mennonites was German (the language they managed to maintain during the hundred years in Russia), it was of great importance that the German language be maintained in this new land. During the early years in Kansas, conducting all schooling in the German language was not a problem. The State allowed and even encouraged the Mennonite people to establish their own schools and curriculum.

However, before many years had passed, the State found it necessary to make English the language to be used for all public education, because it was the official national language. This concerned the Mennonites deeply. "How," they lamented, "will we pass the faith on to our children if they speak the English and we speak the German?" *"Wie sollen wir das machen? Lieber Gott helf uns!"* (What should we do? God help us), and then the plan came. The children would attend the English speaking school sessions as required by the State and, following that, a four to six week session of German school. In German school the children would learn to read and write the German language; they would learn the many stories of the Bible and be able to tell them in German; they would memorize many verses of scripture and the familiar church hymns; they would also be taught the fables, history and other subjects as time allowed.

Thus the beginning of the German Schools came about. (At this writing in 1992 many people in the Western District Conference 60 years and older recall attending German school for one to four years.) This system of schooling the children in both languages worked quite successfully until the world wars, when the surrounding English speaking communities felt hostility toward the people who spoke the German language. It also became increasingly difficult to find teachers who spoke a proper standard High German.

During the years 1934-1935, the Mennonite church of Pretty Prairie, Kansas, was looking for a teacher. The two ladies who had been teaching the German school for a number of years wanted to quit, "But," they told the board, "we have a niece at Inman, Kansas, who might be interested in the job."

Indeed, Mary Thiessen was interested in the job and very flattered, yet humbled, to be offered this opportunity. While Mary was very precise, well-organized and almost perfectionist in her work, she had no formal training in standard High German. She only heard High German in church on Sundays and in daily Bible readings by her father, who probably had the *Plattdeutsch* accent, since that was the only language spoken in Mary's home. Yet Mary just knew she could do this, and it paid thirty dollars plus room and board for the session. Where else could a girl in that day and age, who wanted to go to Hutchinson Juco (the nearby Junior College) in the worst way, ever earn that kind of money?

So with determination to do a good job, the willingness to work as hard as needed to do the job, and much faith that God would go with her, she accepted.

Immediately she began practicing her High German. She listened to the minister's spoken word with new intensity, paying close attention to the usage of words and also to the pronunciation of words. Her father reminded her several times, "You know, Mary, you really don't have much experience speaking the high German. And the Bible stories—do you know 'em good enough to teach 'em?" All of this only made Mary more determined to do the work and do it well.

When the first day arrived, Mary's car was packed with the necessary supplies. In her mind, she had rehearsed over and over everything she planned to do the first day. She even rehearsed every word she planned to say, because she was going to make sure the pupils in her school would be able to pronounce every word correctly. As she drove along the dusty road, she prayed for guidance, and it seemed a surge of hope and confidence filled her until she turned onto the road where the schoolhouse stood. A car approaching from the opposite direction caught her eye. It slowed, pulling into the schoolyard just ahead of her. In it were members of the school board coming to greet her and observe her teaching. "Oh no," she panicked, "this will be the shortest teaching career anyone ever had. They'll know I can't speak the High German. I'll have to resign, and my family will be disgraced." Tears welled up in her eyes. Swallowing hard, she forced her thoughts to the children who would be anxious to meet their new teacher. "I will make it work at least for one day. Then, if they want to fire me, they can. This will be my plan. I will say as few words as possible, only those I know well. It will take time for introductions and seating arrangements, then I'll ask the students to write or memorize verses."

After what seemed an eternity, the school board left. The rest of the day proceeded much as she had planned. That evening Mary waited for the inevitable visit telling her she was not qualified to teach at the school, but no one came so she busily prepared herself for the next day, thinking maybe they would give her a week and give themselves time to find a new teacher. Friday came and went without a word.

Putting aside her fears, she poured her energies into the daily work of making lesson plans, perfecting her own German, and correcting ever-so-gently the children's usage of the language. The children loved this enthusiastic new teacher and she loved them. The playground seemed to be the testing ground for using the High German language. These children spoke *Switzerdeutsch* in their homes and in the excitement of playing softball *die Haussprache* seemed to flourish. However, Mary would gently correct them as best she could considering the enthusiasm for the game, shown especially by one little fellow who even gave every single player on both teams a famous baseball player's name and then insisted that each be called by his famous name during the game.

In the classroom, Mary worked with the children, teaching them the language and encouraging them to memorize as many Bible verses, stories, and hymns as possible. She hoped to give them skills for life in the faith and also prepare them with enough Bible knowledge and memorized verses for the last day of school. "The final day of my teaching career," Mary thought. "Well, I must not dwell on personal matters; I must prepare the children for the big contest." And so she did.

The last day came. All the parents and even some grandparents came for the festive occasion. Mary's heart was heavy knowing this would be the day they would tell her of the dismissal. She exchanged conversation with several board members, but nothing was said. The high point of the day arrived—the contest was about to begin. Parents against children. Whoever could answer the most verses from memory would be this year's winner. The time came for them to line up, children on one side, parents on the other. It was as Mary made her way to the front to be moderator of the contest that she overheard the remark of one of the board members who had visited that first day of school, "I wonder how a teacher of so few words will handle the job of moderator."

Mary Thiessen Goering continued as teacher at the Pretty Prairie German School for six years until 1940. The school closed, never to open again, when she had to resign because she and her husband David were expecting their first child.

Vignettes from Experiences of WDC Congregations

EARLY SUNDAY SCHOOL HISTORY

by Rosella Wiens Regier

The History Gathering Project
[To tell the story of early Sunday school history in the Western District Conference, Rosella Regier invited congregations to share their memories. Approximately 50 individuals, from at least two dozen congregations, contributed material which Rosella combined, together with information she gleaned from her research, to form a series of vignettes that tell the story of Sunday school experiences in the Western District Conference. She grouped most of the material into scenes, naming the individuals whose words she adapted for each skit, making a format useful for groups who want to act out the stories.]

WDC Education Committee Prepares for Centennial Celebrations
(Three people sit in a restaurant, making plans.)

Rosella Regier: I could ask church people to send me stories about their Sunday school experiences. Then I could write skits that could be read or acted out all over the district.

Bertha Harder: What a gift that would be for our children! Imagine what an opportunity this will be for one generation to pass on the faith stories to the next generation.

Earl Sears: I'm reminded of Psalms 78: "...things that we have heard and known, that our fathers have told us. We will not hide them from our children but tell to the coming generation the glorious deeds of the Lord, and of his might, and the wonders which he has wrought...."

Publishing in the General Conference

1991. It is now 110 years since the Department of Publication of the General Conference Mennonite Church began publishing materials!

From the start, the family was seen as the most important avenue for religious education. Parents were to be given "all possible assistance, encouragement, and direction in this most holy work." Of course the Bible was the foundation for all religious efforts in all settings, and the Sunday school and the catechetical instruction became the primary means of supplying Christian education.

Our conference provided materials for churches for a variety of reasons, a major one being a lack of uniformity of materials available from 17 different publishing houses. This diversity was seen as a problem.

What materials did the General Conference publish?

<u>1885:</u> *Der Kinderbote*, a German Sunday school paper.

<u>1889:</u> *Sonntagschul Lektionen fur Jung und Alt*, monthly German Sunday school lessons.

<u>1901:</u> *Sunday School Bible Lessons Quarterly*, first English lessons, was discontinued in 1905; once again published in 1937.

<u>1948:</u> *Mennonite Junior Quarterly* and *Mennonite Young People's Quarterly* introduced.

<u>1952:</u> *Living Faith Graded Sunday School Lessons* by the General Conference were produced together with The Mennonite Church's *Living Faith Sunday School Outlines*. It was a three-year cycle curriculum for children.

<u>1977:</u> *The Foundation Series* for children, and later for youth and adults, became the adopted curriculum for the conference.

<u>1989:</u> Discussion began for a new Anabaptist children's curriculum, which is in process now.

Tabor Mennonite Church
(A circle of six women and two men. Women have hankies with pennies tied into a corner. An offering plate is needed, and other props, as mentioned.)

Ben F. Voth: Our church motto in the early days was from I Cor. 14:40: "Let all things be done decently and in order." No wonder we started Sunday school when we started the church. Our church thought it was important to meet in small groups to study the Word of God.

Art Schmidt: I heard they had the Sand Creek Sunday school back in 1895 before we ever had our building, when we were still called South Alexanderwohl.

Irma Koehn: Oh yes. My Aunt Marie taught her Sunday school class for the Schoentahl group in Low German. Aunt Marie was the oldest sister of Margaret Voth, who still lives at the Bethesda Home in Goessel.

Young children didn't know the English language before they went to school. Even though High German was used in church, it was Low German that was used at home. So that's how the children learned.

Erna Janzen: Do you remember those little story books we got when we memorized verses? Well, at home, Mother would read the story to us in High German as it was printed, and then she'd tell us the story in *Plattdeutsch* so we could understand it.

Bertha A. Schroeder: Do you remember those big teaching pictures that teachers used? The kind that fit on a rod like you sometimes see with maps? They were fairly large.

Ben: At least 3x5 feet.

LuEtta Frey: Is this what you're talking about? (shows picture roll)

Bertha: Yes. That's exactly it. I haven't seen one of those in years. I wonder if my two favorite pictures are there? One was Jesus carrying the lost sheep home, and the other was Jesus sitting on a boulder, blessing the children clustered around him.

Ben: When I was a child, our picture roll was always hung on a blackboard or on an easel stand.

Helen Schmidt: And I remember them in German...I wonder if any of those are still around?

Irma: Yes. There's one here on the table. But it's pretty tattered now.

Art: I want to change the subject. The children were so bashful back then, there probably weren't any discipline problems.

LuEtta: Well, I don't know about that. When I was quite young, maybe around 1933, we met in the kitchen area of the church basement. It was rather dark in that corner, and we sat on the kitchen built-ins. Some boys in the class were quite rowdy and they'd kick their shoes against the shelves. They weren't too good! But Mrs. Peter Frey—she was a good teacher.

Helen: Oh, my yes. Mrs. Frey was a SUPER teacher. She must have held our class spellbound, for I don't recall that there were any discipline problems.

Bertha Schroeder: Sometimes it was awfully hard to keep your attention on the teacher. It was hard to hear her, and we were curious about what was happening on the other side of the curtain. We didn't have regular rooms, just cubicles made by those green burlap curtains. We'd push them back against the wall along the wires when Sunday school was over.

Erna: Something else I remember is that we memorized a lot of Bible verses and sang memorized German songs.

Anna C. Schmidt: And we always took a collection in each class. We little girls proudly untied the corner of our handkerchiefs where we had tied our pennies and put them in the collection plate.

Early Sunday School History

Helen: Let's take that offering now. And we have to sing, "Dropping, Dropping, Dropping."

All: (Women untie penny from hankie. Art Schmidt passes the collection plate as all sing: "Dropping, dropping, dropping/Hear the pennies fall./Everyone for Jesus./He must have them all."

First Mennonite Church, Geary, Oklahoma—by Helen Lehmann
(Two teens, wearing jeans, are reading from old papers)

One: Can you believe this? Our First Mennonite Church here in Geary, Oklahoma, began on a farm in a barn loft!

Two: Barn loft?

One: Yeah. It says it was the barn loft on the J. S. Krehbiel farm.

Two: Here it says that his dad, Christian Krehbiel, gave money for a building to be used for mission work with the Indians. Is that where Mennoville is now?

One: I think so.

Two: Wow! Here's something else. In 1898, J. S. Krehbiel was asked to hold union Sunday schools, together with the Mennonite Sunday school. And get this! He used a store building under construction as a meeting place, and he laid boards across nail kegs and beer barrels for the benches.

One: Beer barrels and nail kegs! In a Mennonite Sunday school?

Buhler Mennonite Church
(Woman, sitting and looking at a church photo)

Martha Wiens: I was in the beginners' Sunday school class when Buhler Mennonite Church was organized in 1920. It was a beautiful church. Our class met in the right hand corner of the church. It had curtains strung on wires on two sides, pulled back for the church service. We had many good times in that class. (looks off into the distance)

Alexanderwohl Mennonite Church

(D. C. Wedel, stands at a podium, reading from his history of Alexanderwohl. Three women on the platform listen intently.)

Wedel: In spite of the fact that Sunday School was designed for religious instruction, it had no easy entry into the Alexanderwohl community. Suspicious of American ways, this innovation was regarded as an intrusion into well-established customs. Since religious instruction was included in all of the area public schools, there was no particular felt need for additional religious instruction.

Early worship was conducted in the Immigrant House, and by 1886 the first church building was erected. By 1880 the church had four scattered Sunday schools held in school houses and by 1898 there were 13, with 441 persons participating and 40 teachers helping. It should be noted that in Alexanderwohl the Sunday school began outside the church.

Velda Duerksen: I asked some of the older members to share memories about early Sunday school classes, and invariably they mentioned Mrs. Helena Warkentine as being their favorite teacher. They said she had a unique way of making the lessons interesting, and they enjoyed the stories she shared.

One story she told that I recall vividly was about the ordeals her family experienced when they joined the group traveling East from Russia into Central Asia, anticipating the second coming of Christ there. She related how they had to wander from one place to another in search of a place where they would be welcome and safe to settle down. She told of the extreme suffering her mother endured when she became ill and then died while they were crossing a desert on camels, and how they had to bury her in this hostile setting and continue on to their destination. I have read many accounts about this ill-fated venture led by Claas Epp, but none have been as impressive as hearing Mrs. Warkentine tell her story in our Sunday school class at Alexanderwohl.

Ruth Schmidt Unruh: I'm a member at Goessel Mennonite Church, but as a young child, I grew up in the Alexanderwohl

Church. My story is about my dad, Gerhard Schmidt, and his brother Wilhelm. They grew up in Alexanderwohl, too.

Sister Esther Schmidt, my cousin, told me a humorous story about my dad and his brother Wilhelm when they were young boys in about 1895. One Sunday morning Gerhard and Wilhelm couldn't find the garters that held up their knee socks. Of course, their mother didn't know about this. That Sunday, as usual, Grandma sat with the smaller children in the back of the church at Alexanderwohl. Grandpa sat up on the stage where Gerhard and Wilhelm sat with him. Grandma was so proud to see her sons up there, singing so heartily and listening so attentively. Suddenly, she saw the binder twine used in place of garters to hold up their socks, and she was very embarrassed.

Judy Unruh: My story is from the early '40s. Children were allowed to go to Sunday school when they were three years old. One of the teachers at that time was Mrs. Minnie Unruh. She had a wonderful smile and such an engaging personality that the children loved her a great deal. When the congregation would gather for the opening, she would go along the back of the church where the young mothers sat and literally gather up the children. She didn't care if we were three years old or just two—if we were willing to go with her, we were welcome. I was one who went with her eagerly. I can still see her at the back of the church, welcoming the little ones. She would usually carry one and have another by the hand with several others following.

Grace Hill Mennonite Church
(Three women are drinking coffee at Kidron-Bethel in North Newton.)

Dorothy Schmidt: It's nice to be together to reminisce about our childhood at Gnadenberg, our Grace Hill Church now. Do you remember when most of the children could speak only the Low German dialect, and Sunday school was conducted in High German? My parents talked High German, so to us children it was no problem, but my, it was sure different then.

Clara Schmidt: Yes. We lived a mile west of the church and I remember how my father and I walked to church many times even when the weather was cold. My primary class met in a rather small room with about 25 to 30 children present. Because we didn't have chairs to sit on we had to stand. Can you believe that? And after walking to church?

Elsie Harms: What I remember is that tap bell on the Sunday school superintendent's table. Do you remember that? (All nod.) He tapped that bell for the classes to close. Children hurried back to their parents. Then the congregation sang and an older person in the audience gave a closing prayer.

Eden Mennonite Church, Moundridge, Kansas
(Two men standing by a pickup truck, on the Eden church yard.)

Paul Zerger: Say, Martin, did you get a letter about finding some material on our Sunday school here at the church?

Martin: Yes, and I hope it's not too late to send it in. I got information from two of our older members and I'd like to have it used.

Paul: Well, what can we say? I know that we were first called Hoffnungsfeld-Eden, but that was later changed to Eden Mennonite Church. We built our first church in 1899.

Martin: That's true. That church had separate entrances for men and women, and they sat on opposite sides of the church. They say the people always knelt for congregational prayer.

Paul: I remember that after Sunday school a bell would ring, signaling all the young children to their parents. Teenage boys sat in the front benches on the men's side. If the boys did not behave in the worship service, the older men in the benches behind them would pull their hair or ear, and the matter was corrected. Of course, the girls never misbehaved!

Martin: Way back, they say, Sunday school was for men only; later, classes were added for women and children. All the children's classes were assigned to the front benches of the sanctuary. The arrangement was to have one or two empty benches between classes.

First Mennonite Church, Beatrice Nebraska
(Church Historical Committee is sitting around a table.)

Hildegard Jantzen: A storyteller for the Western District in the Centennial Year celebrations wants to know about our First Mennonite Church Sunday school beginnings. What can we tell her?

Mrs. Alfred Penner: Well, immigrants came here in 1876.

Mrs. Robert Enz: Even though they hadn't had Sunday school in Europe, they weren't lacking in Christian education.

Mrs. Penner: At first, in 1877, Rev. Heinrich Zimmerman invited the young people to his home for religious instruction on Sunday afternoons.

Hildegard: Yes, and the classes were so well attended that they had to find assistants to help him.

Mrs. Enz: By 1902, they moved the classes into the church—but still on Sunday afternoons.

Mrs. Penner: Look at what I've found here in the history: "In 1905, some of the leaders felt more people would be reached if Sunday school would be held in connection with the Sunday morning services. Adult classes were also started."

Hildegard: That was 28 years after the church was started!

First Mennonite Church, Halstead, Kansas
(Husband and wife sitting in rockers looking at the church centennial book, *The Flock and the Kingdom*.)

Ed Geist: Ruth, I'm sure glad First Mennonite here at Halstead has this centennial book, *The Flock and the Kingdom*.

Ruth Geist: Yes, since you and I didn't grow up in this church it helps us understand the history better, doesn't it?

Ed: I've heard that people here like to think that our congregation was one of the very first to be concerned about having a Sunday school.

Ruth: It says here that in 1876 the constitution included items about Sunday school.

Ed: Listen to this: "All officers of the Sunday school shall work together in harmony." That's from an 1877 addition to the constitution.

Ruth: Here's more from that same year: "The congregation invites all Sunday school friends in or out of the congregation to participate in the Sunday school."

Ed: Here's something else that's interesting. The book talks about fond memories. And one of them is about the annual Sunday school picnic: "The annual Sunday school picnic is an event of significance for all members. The first such event recorded was scheduled as the celebration of the *Kinderfest* in the *walde* (woods) on Ascension Day, May 15, 1880." But I want you to hear the list of committees:

        Program Committee
        Croquet, Ring, and Horseshoe Committee
        Swing Committee
        Bread Committee
        Play Committee
        Place and Water Committee
        Committee for Boat Rides

Ruth: Whoever said we're more organized now than they were in the early days?

Ed: Oh, one more thing: "Bad weather forced postponement of the big event to Pentecost Monday!"

First Church of Christian, Moundridge, Kansas
(Teenager and his mother are seated at the kitchen table with books and papers scattered about.)

Jon Goering: Mom, I gotta work on this report about our church for catechism class. You know more about it than I do. Wanna help?

Gladys Goering: Twisting my arm, right? Okay then. What's first?

Jon: Let's just list a bunch of facts about First Church of Christian here at Moundridge.

Gladys: For starters, the church began in 1876.

Jon: And this church and the Halstead church were together.

Gladys: And Sunday school started in 1876, too.

Jon: How do you know that?

Gladys: Here's some early history: "...the suggestion of the minister of the congregation met with approval, that the matter of an immediate introduction to Sunday school be discussed. The unopposed progress of a business meeting proved that this was a suggestion FROM THE LORD. As a result the Sunday school was opened and introduced with special festivities on the second day of Christmas of the same year, 1876."

Jon: Okay, what else?

Gladys: Well, till 1878, the two churches alternated Sundays— Church worship on Sunday and a morning of Sunday school on the next Sunday. At that point, the two churches separated into two congregations.

132 Stories of Remembrance & Restoration

<u>Jon</u>: Anything else before I start writing?

<u>Gladys</u>: Just one more thing. When you were early school age, your class was put into the choir loft. That was a strategic error! Every wiggle—and there were plenty—was seen by the entire congregation.

<u>Jon</u>: Aw, Mom!

Emmaus Mennonite Church, Whitewater, Kansas
(Woman sitting at a desk, browsing through church records.)

<u>Elsie Claassen</u>: As church statistician, I know these facts are important. But I need to connect facts to something real, something that made a difference in our church. Let's see:

— We came from West Prussia in 1876, met in homes at first.
— Dedicated a church building in 1877.
— First catechism class was baptized in 1877.

That means classes were held from the very beginning. Interesting!

— 1904: bought German song books and decided Sunday school would be held from 9:30-10:30.
— 1956: graded series of lesson materials were introduced, so we needed more classrooms.

Here's something:

— 1916: "The Sunday school superintendent asked the Elder whether any of the four candidates for baptism were eligible for Sunday school teachers. He recommended that all four were good prospects."

There's my interesting connection. I know about those four; two of them taught for 20 or more years, one was the church organist, and the only boy became teacher, superintendent, and finally a deacon in the church. The Lord does work!

A Women in Mission Program at Western District Conference
Churches: West Zion, Meno, Bethel/Inman, Friedenstahl/Tampa, Bergthal/Pawnee Rock
(In a row of chairs, one program moderator and five speakers are seated on a platform, ready to contribute their part. Bertha Galle needs a Bible story picture card.)

Moderator of WM Program: Thank you all for coming to our evening program. Our guests are all over 75 years of age, and each will share a special memory about her Sunday school experience when she was very young. Mrs. Galle, please go ahead.

Bertha Galle: My church is West Zion in Moundridge, Kansas. We were organized in 1888 and started Sunday school just two months after beginning services. When I was a child, the Bible stories were taught with each child receiving a small card with a Bible story picture on the front and the story on the back. Here's one of mine. (holds up old picture card)

Moderator: Thank you, Bertha. Mrs. Becker?

Iola Becker: I'm from the Meno Mennonite Church, Meno, Oklahoma. We had Sunday school according to age. We were sometimes assigned songs. We had to learn to read and sing the notes instead of the words. It did sound a little funny to sing only the notes.

Moderator: Interesting, Iola! Mrs. Pauls, are you ready?

Lena Pauls: I talked with Mrs. P. T. Neufeld. We are both members at the Bethel Mennonite Church at Inman, Kansas. We remember that at first in our church, there were only men teachers, and they were chosen by the men. Probably the thought prevailed that a "woman should be silent in the church." I remember going to the front of the church, boys on one side and girls on the other side. And I remember my uncle Abraham Toews was teaching. Another uncle who taught us was John H. Toews. He was killed in an accident in 1912, and that made quite an impression on me.

Moderator: Thanks, Lena. Now Linda Richert, please.

Linda Richert: I grew up in the Friedenstahl Mennonite Church in rural Tampa, Kansas. At first, we met in a one-room school house that was heated with a pot-bellied coal stove. Each Sunday a different member of the church would go to church early to start the fire, so the building would be warm by the time the rest of us arrived.

Most of the families came to church in a horse-drawn carriage. We were fortunate to have a hood over ours. There were ten in our family, and we all fit into one carriage. We did this by having the older children hold the smaller children on their laps. Other families came in horse-drawn spring wagons.

It took us at least 30 minutes to go three miles to church. Mother got real nervous when we took the high-spirited horse, so my father always chose the slowest horse to take us to church. This, of course, displeased us children.

One more thing. When we got Bible story pictures to take home, we were so proud of them we would put them on our walls. We didn't have any other decorations in our home except these Bible story pictures.

Moderator: That was beautiful, Linda. Thank you for sharing. Maxlyn Smith, are you next?

Maxlyn Smith: In 1875, the first Bergthal Mennonite Church at Pawnee Rock was built of limestone block from a nearby quarry. Because people were so scattered they met alternately at the church, in a schoolhouse, and in a home.

As long as anyone can remember, Christmas Eve was celebrated in church with a program by the Sunday school classes. As the church grew, more and more children struggled through their recitations and songs until the program was so long that it started at 7 p.m. and lasted until after 10 p.m. Perhaps they did not use Christmas trees in the old stone church, but after the frame church was built in 1899, they did. The early trees were trimmed with popcorn and paper chains and lighted candles. Some stories say one man, others say four men, stood near the tree with buckets of water and sponges tied to poles in case the tree caught on fire. Later, after the brick church was built, tall trees were specially ordered for the church. Unless the tree was sixteen feet tall and touched the ceiling, some people complained that it was too short.

Of course, one of the greatest features of the Christmas Eve program was the treats.

Moderator: Well, those were wonderful stories. Thank you all for sharing.

Bethel Mennonite Church, Hydro, Oklahoma
(A woman talking to children during a worship service story time.)

Wilma McKee: Today I want to tell you some stories about the children who have grown up in our Bethel Mennonite Church here at Hydro, Oklahoma.

Once upon a time, several children in this church had whooping cough. They didn't want to miss Sunday school. So you know what they did? They parked a car behind the church and all the sick children were taught in that car. I was one of those children.

Child: Is that really true? (Wilma nods.)

Wilma: In this church, the children always memorized lots of Bible verses. Sometimes they memorized by rote, and the words didn't make very good sense to the small children. One day all the children had to say a Bible verse from memory to the whole congregation. One little girl said: "When people leaved their houses, they lock their doors." Since that sentence isn't in the Bible, the people laughed.

One of the children: Can you tell us another one?

Wilma: This story is about my Aunt Anna Entz. When she was about five years old, she sat on a church bench, but her feet didn't reach the floor. So she sat there, and she'd swing and swing her feet back and forth as her legs hung from the seat of the bench.

Finally, her father came over from the men's side of the church and carried her back with him. She said it was so embarrassing to have to go sit with the men.

Another child: Did the men really all sit on one side?

Wilma: Yes, they did.
    This next story happened to a little girl in our church whom you all know. We were having a special church celebration at Bethel church recently, so we had worship services, but we skipped Sunday school. This one little girl was heart broken and refused to leave the church until her teacher took her to their classroom for a short little visit. I'm glad those of us here at Bethel Mennonite Church consider Sunday school important, aren't you?

A Child: Did I say that, Wilma? Who was that little girl? (Wilma just smiles.)

Wilma: All of you know Roy Dick in our church. He's about retirement age now. But when he was a little boy, my mother, Elsie Entz, was his teacher. She taught those little children here for over 30 years. You remember that she died recently. Well, on the day of her funeral Roy Dick wrote a poem in her memory and brought it to our house.

Hebron Mennonite Church, Buhler, Kansas; Inman Mennonite Church, Inman, Kansas; and Hoffnungsau, Inman, Kansas
(Two men and two women are sitting together drinking coffee)

Ray Regier: I was reading early Hebron church records. In 1882 they built our first church building in just 30 days. Can you imagine that—just 30 days?

Albert Ediger: We moved into the new large frame building of our Hoffnungsau church in 1898. That's when they started having Sunday school classes in the church. When our church was organized in 1875, we didn't have Sunday school classes. Leaders knew that neighboring churches were having Sunday school, but they wanted everyone to favor this move with no quarreling.

> *A Thank You for a Special Teacher*
>
> by Roy Dick—one of your many students
>
> Thank you for the warmth that kept us from feeling the physical cold in the Cradle Roll classroom.
>
> Thank you for your patience shown to boys and girls who constantly swung their feet from too tall benches and made strange requests for special songs to be sung.
>
> Thank you for security which you gave us when all around there was poverty.
>
> Thank you for creating a closeness in our class for one another and for you. "Elsie" was always a fitting title.
>
> Thank you for motivating us with cards, large posters, attendance sheets and in more subtle ways.
>
> Thank you for helping us to learn that good teachers are caring people. Your care then and throughout our lives has always been there.
>
> Thank you for modeling the concept that "love endures forever."
>
> Thank you for helping us understand the comfort that comes to us now as we lean on your Jesus.

<u>Ruth Wiens</u>: People who later formed our Inman Mennonite Church first worshipped at Hoffnungsau. That was 14 miles for some people. Some of them traveled by buggy or even riding on grain-drills, so they started Sunday schools in nearby schools, like Big Lake and Blaze Fork schools.

<u>Ray</u>: At Hebron, we started having Sunday school before we had church services regularly. On a scrap of paper in a box of church papers it says: "Had Sunday school before Father Buhler came" as leader or pastor.

Amanda Bartel: I learned values that must have come both from Sunday school and from my home. That says a lot about the Christian education program at Hoffnungsau.

I remember one summer when Irene Sperling broke her leg and couldn't come to church. Our teacher, Lena Penner Schmidt (now from Alexanderwohl), arranged for us to go to her home for class. Mrs. Sperling had inverted a chair to form a backrest for Irene, and there she lay in a comfortable position with pillows all around her for support. The attention she got was almost enviable.

I have among my prized possessions a set of bud vases, a gift Lena gave to each of her girls that Christmas.

For Children's Day, Lena had us do a reading that used a rainbow for a prop; I can still see the beautiful crepe paper rainbow that stood behind us as we spoke our lines.

Another teacher, Martha Unruh Siemens, led us girls in good discussions, but the thing I remember most was a potluck that she suggested we have on a Friday night. My sister coached me in making a macaroni dish that went over big; it also improved my self esteem.

Ruth: At Inman Mennonite, the Sunday school picnic was the big event. After a busy afternoon of baseball and other games, everyone was treated to a dish of "boughten" ice cream.

Ray: Oh yes. And you had to say "boughten," not "bought."

Albert: In our adult classes at Hoffnungsau, we'd often sit in the second and third bench rows and the teacher would stand in the first row and teach. Very little discussion took place; they mostly explained, and very few questions were asked. This system changed as new teachers came and adults began participating. One class member made this remark: "I like Sunday school because we talk of all kinds of things—world news and what's going on in our different churches and community, and we apply the lesson to our daily living."

Ray: I want to mention another interesting fact about Hebron. I have a letter written by Sam Regier to his "folks," in 1927 that says: "Last Thursday the Kansas-Nebraska Sunday school convention took place at our church. A tent was put up. We served lunch for the whole bunch. About 1,000 people were there."

<u>Albert</u>: It seems to me there was a strong sense of Christian nurturing in our Inman-Buhler churches.

First Mennonite Church, Clinton, Oklahoma
(Ninety-two year-old man sitting in a rocker, talking to a pastor.)

<u>Jake Klaassen</u>: I'm 92 years old now. Back in 1952 when Clinton decided to work on a new church building, I was chairman of the building committee.

<u>Walter H. Regier</u>: Jake, I heard that earlier you moved an older schoolhouse into town to serve as the church.

<u>Jake</u>: That's right. And we thought Sunday school was so important that we put some walls into that school building so we'd have classrooms. That worked until the building was too small.

<u>Walter</u>: Charles Regier, a member for 36 years, remembers that the youth were promised their own classroom in the new building. So the youth helped with the decking and nailed it with 10-inch spikes.

<u>Jake</u>: Yes, that's right.

<u>Walter</u>: Another thing people said was that God gave the church a miracle with finances. Everyone shared a dollar a week in the offering once a month, and they gathered $1,800 that way. Later someone else gave $5,000 to finish off the $35,000 total cost.

<u>Jake</u>: A lot of the people hadn't been Mennonites very long. They'd been Lutheran, Federated, Mennonite Brethren, and General Conference. But we all worked together to build our church.

Stories of Remembrance & Restoration

Lorraine Avenue Mennonite Church, Wichita, Kansas
(Seven women meet for coffee in a mall in Wichita to discuss the Sunday school experience at Lorraine Avenue church.)

<u>Ruth Harms Wiebe</u>: I remember when this part of Wichita was almost open prairie.

<u>Frieda Unrau</u>: That's true. I worked as a domestic along Hillside when I was young. Our preacher, C. E. Krehbiel, used to bring my boyfriend, Clarence Unrau, along from Newton, when he came here. That's a long time ago.

<u>Mary Janzen</u>: I think the Lorraine Avenue church was organized in 1933. I remember back to 1936, but Sunday school had probably started two years before that. Frieda Frey and I taught the kindergarten class in a little spot near the furnace in the basement of the parsonage church.

One time our daughter, Myrna, was in Minnie Gaeddert's group and she wouldn't stay in class. Minnie had a way of dealing with that; she told Myrna she needed her to pass the collection plate and that solved the problem.

<u>Kathryn Galle Vogt</u>: I was a charter member of the church. I remember we met in the John Mueller house, the second building that we used for church and Sunday school. Agnes Warkentin was my teacher then. She was a strong leader in Christian education till she died in 1960.

<u>Ruth</u>: Back in 1936, I taught a class of third graders under the rafters in the second story of the parsonage church. How different it was in the 1980s.

<u>Amanda Bartel</u>: Ruth, that means you've taught at Lorraine for nearly 50 years.

<u>Ruth</u>: It doesn't seem that long because I enjoyed it so much.

<u>Lucille Schmidt Phillips</u>: I remember when our teacher, Agnes Warkentin, took our Junior High class to Sim Park where we

cooked a pancake breakfast on an open fire. After a nature lesson, we all went back to church.

Lucille: Yes, and I can still visualize the delicate sandwiches she made in the shape of lilies.

Mary Ann: Vena Stucky was my favorite teacher. Our class met in a curtained-off space in the basement of the parsonage church building. For special times, our class went to different members' homes and played games in the yard.

Lucille: Remember, Mary Ann, when we teamed up to teach the three-year-olds for several years?

Mary Ann: We must have appreciated our childhood Sunday school to take over like that.

Amanda: You've talked about all the little extras that teachers put into their work with children. All of the experiences together really make up the value system that is obviously a part of you, even today—50 and 60 years later.

Arvada Mennonite Church, Arvada Colorado, and Mennonite Church of the Servant, Wichita, Kansas

(A man and a woman are each on a phone at opposite ends of the room, talking long distance.)

Tom Mierau: Hello, Donna. This is Tom Mierau. I belong to the Mennonite Church of the Servant in Wichita. We got a letter asking for information about early Sunday school in our church. We're not a very old church—about 15 years, so I thought I'd call someone with a little longer history to see how you're going to answer the letter.

Donna: I'm the historian here at Arvada Mennonite Church near Denver, so I got the same letter. We've been here about 34 years now, and I've located some early history I'm going to send in.

Tom: What will you say?

<u>Donna</u>: Well, for one thing, we're lucky to have two of the 41 charter members still in our church. Lily Whitsett is 77 now, and I've been talking with her. She said that while the church was being built in 1960, they met for Sunday school classes in a crowded, dreary basement in a nearby school. They were glad to have separate rooms in the new building.

<u>Tom</u>: I can imagine. We're a house church, so we always move around and adapt. We have people who were here at our beginning, too. And I've been reading church minutes and newsletters. I found that the church talked about nurturing children all along.

We tried lots of new forms, too—family clusters, worship designed for kids to participate, and things like that. I think we've been pretty creative through the years in making all our congregational activities conducive to children. Eventually though, we developed traditional classes for children, and that's working quite well now.

<u>Donna</u>: An interesting tradition in our congregation is the annual Christmas program given by the Sunday school children and the adult choir. The manger scene with the children taking the parts of Mary and Joseph, shepherds and the angels, is such a joy for the parents to watch. In fact, right from the start, Lily Whitsett's farm furnished the roughly hewn manger and straw; that manger is still used to this day.

<u>Tom</u>: That sounds exciting. It's been good talking with you, Donna. I think I can write my report now.

Turpin Mennonite Church, Turpin, Oklahoma
(Members are sitting around tables following a potluck meal at the church; 16 people speak.)

<u>Kevin Goertzen</u>: I've been here at Turpin church for only a little while. But I get the feeling there's a lot of history here. Settlers came in 1903, and the first preacher came in 1907. I found that out in the 75th anniversary booklet.

Annie Hiebert: I was here as a kid, and I sure have a lot of memories. Tobe Dirks was my Sunday school teacher, and we all enjoyed him so much.

Katie Siemens: Our church was small, but we managed to have lots of good services. I remember the Sunday school picnics at Sharp's Creek and at the Arkalon Park on the Cimarron River. That was really a treat.

Agatha Wiens Vogt: My father started the first Sunday school here in our dugout. Later a dugout school was made one mile east and one mile north of the present church. That dugout was used for Sunday school, too. One Sunday morning, we came there, and found that dugout full of water. The men fished the benches out and we had Sunday school outside.

Lizzie Dyck: I remember that, too. But I think the dugout was only HALF full of water!

Leona Loepp: Our parents were faithful about taking us to church each Sunday. We never knew if the "Old Ford" would make it, but most of the time it did. Do you remember the bucket of drinking water with the dipper? It was in the little nursery. How good that water tasted! The trips to the nursery to get a drink were suddenly stopped when Dad decided to take a jar of water to church and kept it with him where he sat.

Esther Epp: That brings back memories. We never knew if our Model T Ford would start. When it didn't, Dad would hitch the horses to the wagon and we would go to church.

Joe Hinz: Esther, I might as well say it now. You were my Sunday school teacher for many years. You were the greatest!

Dorothy Janzen Sangals: Marie Plett was our Sunday school teacher, and we loved her dearly. I'm sure the things she taught have had a permanent influence in my life. One of the special things she did for us was to take us to Liberal, Kansas, so we could attend a Catholic Mass. It helped us see the difference in types of services.

Johnny Dirks: I don't remember who my first teacher was, but we would receive a Bible verse on a card a little larger than a postage stamp.

Mary Ann Boese Becker: I often taught Sunday school. Those small children were always so ready to learn the Bible stories and to memorize Bible verses.

LaVerle Dirks Schrag: One of my Sunday school memories is a reward of a little bee pin for learning the beatitudes.

Phyllis Isaacs Kliewer: I have very pleasant memories of my early church experiences. Sure, I watched the clock, whispered and read my Sunday school papers during preaching, but it's very good having such a heritage and I'm the richer for it. I shared my memories with my nine-year-old and she said, "Mom, you really liked church, didn't you?" She's right.

Vernon Plett: I remember when the young people wanted a Sunday school room and they dug out a room under the southwest corner of the church. It took a lot of work, but it was worth it.

Gary Franz: Oh, yes. We used a dirt bucket that was pulled by a tractor outside the church, thus pulling the dirt through a small opening in the existing foundation. When the walls were finally in, we made some of the corners rounded rather than square. Our sponsor jokingly commented that "the devil can't corner us in this room!" We also built a table about as big as the room for our discussions. We marveled at our workmanship and experienced deep satisfaction at our ability to create such a nice place for our class to meet.

Raylene Hinz Penner: My very earliest church memories are as a child some 25 years ago: the tall Christmas tree in the corner, goodie sacks at the door on Christmas Eve, coffee smells and wonderful food aromas arising out of the basement, scuffing my "Sunday" shoes on the sidewalk on my way to the outdoor toilet, and getting in trouble for sliding down those pipe rails.

I listened over the years as I grew up, and my training in the Turpin Church is one of my most valued treasures. I learned the Bible, and it has stayed with me. We all got to participate and that was invaluable experience for me. The many words of encouragement had to be instrumental in the formulation of a strong self-concept.

Our family life centered around Turpin Church; the people in the church were our friends, fellow believers and fellow workers for the values which held us together. Something of that kind of influence stays with one a lifetime, I believe. Throughout my life, on Sunday mornings, I'll recall the meadowlarks singing and reflecting our morning joy and reverence as our family headed the car south to worship at Turpin Mennonite Church.

Early Sunday School Experiences
(An interview with <u>Ruth Schmidt Unruh</u>)

My parents, Gerhard and Louise Schmidt, were members at the Alexanderwohl Mennonite Church just north of Goessel, Kansas, and I attended there off and on as a child until I was about eight years old. At that time, in 1920, the Goessel Mennonite Church was built, and my parents became charter members there.

My earliest Sunday school memories are of the Alexanderwohl Church in the years before I went to school. My Sunday school class was held in an entrance room, just outside the sanctuary. That's the room where the mothers with small babies sat to care for the children during church. In that room, behind a curtain, was our class. There were between 50 and 60 children there every Sunday—all tiny preschoolers. We sat on backless benches! I remember we used the large flip charts with Bible story pictures and Bible verses.

I remember the names of some of my teachers from before I was five years old. One was Mrs. David Schmidt. She was a good storyteller and could relate to children. Another one was Agnes Unruh Reimer who is Shelly Buller's grandmother. My aunt, Agnes Schmidt Funk also taught our class.

Our class was conducted in Low German. High German was the official language for the worship service then, but since most of the children spoke Low German at home and were comfortable in that language, that's what was used in Sunday school. Of course, there was always a Bible story.

Then we had to learn a Bible verse in High German. It was called a *Spruch*. The teacher gave us a tiny card (they have them on display at the Goessel Museum) on which was printed the Bible verse and the scripture reference. These tiny cards came on large perforated sheets. Each of us children took home that Bible verse card so we could learn the verse during the week. We came back to Sunday school the next Sunday and recited the verse for the teacher. After we had learned 10 verses, we returned our 10 Bible verse cards in exchange for a High German story book. I still have some of mine. The titles in English are: *Stories for Young and Old, Out of All the World, Jack the Flower Friend.* How we children loved the stories in those books. After Sunday dinner, Mother would read the stories to herself and then tell us children the stories in low German. We couldn't wait until she finished reading them to herself. We'd beg and beg for her to tell us one of the stories.

I still remember many of those verses I learned in High German. Children don't memorize as much today, though they do many other things. But I'm glad I memorized. Those are still precious to me today.

My mother, Louise Lehrman Schmidt, who was born in 1887, told me about Sunday school at Alexanderwohl when it was held on Sunday afternoons in a nearby country school, Green Valley. Her family walked for miles to get there. Sometimes, when they went to church, they took turns going. They were a big family, and it was hard to get everyone ready. Sometimes the older children would stay home with her mother and take care of the little ones. If it was cold, they bundled up with hot bricks and blankets in the wagon.

As far back as I can remember, the Alexanderwohl church was big and crowded. Our home was two-and-a-half miles from the church. It was hard to get there by horse and buggy when it was muddy or cold. Also, some people living in Goessel didn't have transportation. So some of the families started another church service in the Goessel Preparatory School.

My Sunday school class was on the south side of the school, on a platform. My teacher was *Schmita Lanch* (Helen). She's Jan Wedel's grandmother. I always took my little brother to sit with me in Sunday school. I remember that the adults were in the same room for their class, sitting in the school benches. Church was also held in the same room.

As a child, I always looked forward to Children's Day, which was held in summer. For six to eight weeks before the program, we got together to practice for it once a week and toward evening. We children liked to come early and run around and play games before we started practicing. We played things like "Run for your Breakfast," and "Three-Deep."

Regular church was in the morning. Then we quickly went home for dinner. And in the afternoon there was the program. It was long. There would be poems, dialogues, pantomimes and singing. The stage was always decorated with lots of flowers. People would gather them from all over the community, for everyone had flower gardens. It was mostly a High German program with some English. Afterward there would be a "faspa." We'd have the regular things—zweibach, cheese and bologna. Some of the boys would compete to see who could eat the most bologna! In addition we always had special food—ice cream and cookies.

We had a catechism class before baptism. It was a Sunday school class where we memorized the answers to questions in a little book. Just before baptism, there was a special evening when each baptismal candidate gave a testimony, usually sharing a special Bible verse or a song with special meaning. For baptism, earlier, everyone wore black. Ours was the first class to wear white. We were presented a German book, *Words to Young Christians.*

The Conference Grows

CHURCH PLANTING SINCE THE 1950s

by Walt Neufeld

The first era
Among the first city churches started by the Western District was the First Mennonite Church of Hutchinson, begun in 1914 with H. J. Dyck as pastor. Fifteen years later, the Lorraine Avenue Mennonite Church in Wichita, was started, with Arnold E. Funk as pastor. These two congregations represent the first era of city missions outreach.

The second era
The second era of church planting included three congregations, two of them in city locations. In 1935 the WDC city mission efforts started in Oklahoma with the Grace Mennonite Church of Enid. J. B. Frey was pastor. In 1942 the conference began work in Walton, Kansas, with Jacob Enz as pastor. In 1944 the First Mennonite Church in McPherson, Kansas, began with Roland Goering as pastor. We must not overlook the importance of the four city congregations planted from the teens through the forties, for today these churches have an approximate current total membership of 1,113. They represent an important part of our conference membership and work.

During these years much Home Mission Committee effort was directed at supporting rural congregations. As late as 1953 the HMC report to the conference listed congregations such as Ransom, Greensburg, and Kismet in Kansas; Gotebo and Carnegie in Oklahoma; and Vona in Colorado. The First Mennonite Church of Ransom received subsidy from the district as late as 1958.

The dawn of the new era
In the early 1950s many voices in the Western District called for renewed efforts in urban church planting. In part these were motivated by the biblical mandate to "go and preach the gospel." The louder voices were prompted by fear and alarm, when conference leaders and pastors became aware of declining church memberships, declining numbers of farms and farmers, and a rapid move of young people to the cities.

Of course, these voices had been there for some time, but our traditional fear of cities made us reluctant to heed them. As early as 1925, S. M. Grubb had warned about the "steady drift of our own young people to the cities." He said, "There is another situation which we as Mennonites have neglected and which will rise to haunt us to our shame in the future. We have made no provision for keeping these brethren in close touch with the Mennonite Church." A special study committee, composed of John F. Schmidt, J. Winfield Fretz, Howard Nyce, and Leland Harder, reported that in the five year period between 1956 and 1961, the rural congregations in the conference lost a total of 558 members, while the urban congregations gained 497.

In 1965, Dale Brown, at the General Conference sessions at Estes Park, Colorado, said that the rural church was dying and almost dead. The message was very clear: We must build the church in the city whether we like it or not! Some voices cautioned about the motive of going into the cities only to save the "Mennos." But a new era of urban church planting had begun in earnest.

The new vision for and interest in planting urban churches came about, not only because of these fears but also because there was a genuine vision for evangelistic outreach building in our conference. Because of this dual impetus, several things came together that made this effort possible.

In 1955 a resolution was adopted by the conference which authorized the Home Missions Committee to reach out, including "starting of new churches in the cities." Additionally, a Revolving Church Building Fund was established to aid local congregations in building new houses of worship. A resolution was adopted at the 1957 conference making revolving church building funds also available to the Home Missions Committee for use in starting new churches. The third impetus was when the 1957 Conference sessions approved doubling the Home Missions Committee budget from the usual $25,000 per year to $50,000 per year. This dramatic increase in the Home Missions budget came about because the conference was ready for it, and because of the vision of certain people.

Though many could be recognized who made major contributions in WDC church planting, Elbert Koontz and Peter T. Neufeld were two significant people who were a part of my knowledge and experience of the time.

Elbert did not grow up in the Mennonite Church. His parents were both pastors in the Evangelical United Brethren Church. Elbert became an Anabaptist and loyal worker in the Mennonite Church by conviction. He embraced with enthusiasm and loyalty the principles of belief that are central to our faith. When I was just out of seminary and became pastor at the Brudertal Mennonite Church at Hillsboro, Kansas, Elbert Koontz was pastor at the First Mennonite Church there. His mentoring and friendship remain with me still. Elbert was a unique person, always abounding in energy and ideas.

One day when he and I were visiting he told me that he was going to recommend to the Executive Committee that the Western District double the Home Missions budget. I told him, "Elbert, you're nuts—they will never go for it." He sat back in his chair and calmly replied, "I think maybe they will;" and added, "if they don't, that's okay, too." He seemed to have his finger on the pulse of the district and the times. When conference time came, the conference indeed went for it. He was ready to dream new dreams and never feared to act on them. Years later, when he was conference minister and I was president of the conference, we reminisced about that turning point in our conference history. There were many other times and occasions when he proposed new ideas for consideration.

We were all saddened when Elbert was stricken by cancer. Even though his condition rapidly worsened, he continued to perform his conference duties for a time, before he passed away in 1978. He had lived a strong life; the work that he did and many of the ideas he proposed and implemented are still with us, most noticeably the strong interest in planting churches.

Another person who played an important role in the urban church planting effort in the early stages was the Rev. Peter T. Neufeld of Inman. He served two separate terms on the Home Missions Committee, from 1951 to 1954 and again from 1959 to 1962, serving as chairman for several of these years. He was my uncle and also my pastor during my youth at the Bethel Mennonite Church of Inman.

Peter T. Neufeld served as pastor and elder of the Bethel Church for over four decades, most of the time without salary. During his later ministry there, and after he retired from preaching, he spent endless hours exploring urban areas in which the Western District was planning to plant churches. Then he would report on his investigations and effort to acquire property and locations for church planting.

Mennonites have always had a gift for acquiring good land and property, but they were seriously hampered by limited funds. Urban church planting had a rocky start in the fifties and sixties. Being a rural people, we often seemed not to be planting urban churches but planting rural churches in the city. People even suggested that Mennonites might be unable to learn urban church planting and should leave it to others—the Baptists and Methodists who could do it so much better. Yet it was the vision and efforts of people like Elbert Koontz, Peter T. Neufeld, and many others, that began a successful era of urban church planting which remains alive and well today.

Approximately 30 urban churches have been planted since the 1950s. Each planting is a long and interesting story in itself. Space limitations allow only a brief synopsis here.

Third Era—1950s and 1960s—Total current membership, 1,096
<u>Clinton, Oklahoma</u>. The third era of church planting began with the establishment of the First Mennonite Church, Clinton, Oklahoma in 1951, with Henry D. Penner as pastor. The work was

authorized by the Home Missions Committee in 1949. Western District field worker B. H. Janzen, Levi Koehn, and Arthur Isaac served the group on Sundays in 1950. A new bulding was dedicated on November 30, 1958, with 440 people present. The current membership is 112.

Topeka, Kansas. B. H. Janzen explored the possibility of a church in Topeka as early as 1948, but reported slow progress. In 1954, a I-W Fellowship was begun in the city; by 1956 a church was established with Floyd Bartel as the first full time pastor. Mennonite Brethren were a part of this congregation until 1958 when they withdrew and formed their own congregation. Membership is now 101.

Kansas City, Kansas. The Rainbow Boulevard Mennonite Church began August 1, 1957, with Stanley Bohn as pastor. Later this congregation merged with the Grace Mennonite Church, and today is affiliated in local ministry and sharing a building with United Methodist and United Church of Christ congregations. The membership is 176.

Newton, Kansas. A group that began meeting in 1957 in Sister Frieda Chapel under the leadership of W. F. Unruh and Harold Regier, organized in March 1958 as the Faith Mennonite Church. Howard G. Nyce resigned from the Home Missions Committee to become the first full time pastor. Current membership is 375.

Liberal, Kansas. In January 1958, 70 people met to consider starting a church in Liberal. Vern Jantz, a teacher, and his wife Helen, daughter of Peter T. Neufeld, along with Harold Jantzen of the Kismet church, provided early leadership. Harold Jantzen became the first pastor when the church started on April 12, 1959. At present the membership is 58.

Arvada, Colorado. After lengthy exploration of Denver for a suitable site, a church was begun on the northwest side of the city in the suburb of Arvada. Don Wismer became the pastor in September 1957. During 1961, Peter T. Neufeld, member of the Home Missions Committee provided pulpit supply. Later the congregation contributed a substantial amount of money and a number of members to begin the Boulder congregation. Still later the congregation gave support to start the Aurora congregation on the east side of Denver. The Arvada congregation is known throughout the greater Denver area for its strong peace witness. They have 67 members currently.

<u>Oklahoma City, Oklahoma</u>. Interest in establishing a church in Oklahoma City began in 1956. By 1958 a Fellowship was begun with Jake Krause as pastor. This group included a number of Mennonite Brethren people. In 1960 the Mennonite Brethren withdrew, and the work was discontinued. In 1964 O'Ray and Edith Graber and Donald and Elvira Schierling went to Oklahoma City to begin a VS and Community service project. On January 3, 1971, the group merged with the United Presbyterian Chruch to become Trinity Mennonite-Presbyterian Church. After considerable disagreement and dissatisfaction from a few members of the Presbyterian church about the support of the Mennonite Service Unit, this union was dissolved in 1980, in an action that was disappointing to those present at the congregation's last meeting.

<u>Houston, Texas</u>. In 1965, Elmer Friesen, Western District Minister, explored the possibilities of work in the Dallas/Ft. Worth area and the Houston/Galveston area. The work in Houston was begun in 1967, with Elmer Friesen as pastor. Boys and girls clubs, Bible School, and a Track and Field program have been at the center of their local community ministries. Their membership is now 74.

<u>Hesston, Kansas</u>. A group from the Mennonite Church and General Conference backgrounds met to plan something new—a dually affiliated church. The result was the Hesston Inter-Mennonite Church, begun in 1967 with Gideon Yoder as pastor. They have 133 members.

Fourth Era—1970s and 1980s—Total current membership, 840.
<u>Manhattan, Kansas</u>. Interested Mennonites in Manhattan began to meet as early as 1955 under the leadership of Gerald Thierstein, Don Peters, and Martha Stucky. Nothing cohesive developed until Rosie Epp gave leadership during the school year of 1977-78, when a church was started. Michael Claassen became the first full time pastor in mid-1978. This group is affiliated with three

Mennonite conferences—Western District (GC), South Central (MC), and South Central Mennonite Brethren. There are 69 members.

Dallas, Texas. By mid-1976 a group of Mennonites who had been meeting in the Dallas area with John Miller as leader, were accepted into the Western District Conference as the Peace Mennonite Fellowship. The next year Ernest Hershberger was interim minister. Their local ministry and outreach has focused on Peace and Social Concerns. They currently have 46 members.

Lawrence, Kansas. Mennonites with some relationship to the University of Kansas had begun meeting in Lawrence as early as 1949. In 1980 the Home Mission Committee, along with the local group, began the church with John Linscheid as pastor. The current membership is 40.

Ft. Collins, Colorado. In 1973 Mennonites met for monthly potluck dinners and explored possibilities of forming a church. In 1980 they organized under the joint support of the Western District and the Rocky Mountain Mennonite Conference, with David and Norma Gingerich as leaders. Their membership is 40.

Salina, Kansas. In 1981 the Salina Mennonite Church was begun with Eldon Epp as pastor. This new venture was supported jointly by the Western District and a "mother" church, the Eden Mennonite Church of Moundridge, Kansas. Fifteen years earlier an attempt had been made to start a church in Salina, but the local group was not ready for such a venture then. Present membership is 33.

Dallas, Texas. The Home Missions Committee started the Iglesia Cristiano Mennonita church in 1982. Tony Arevalo and his family came from Colombia, South America, to provide leadership for this congregation. Part of their ministry has been to Spanish-speaking recent immigrants from Mexico. They have 38 members.

Palmer Lake, Colorado. The Colorado Springs Mennonite Church helped organize the congregation at Palmer Lake. The Rocky Mountain Mennonite Conference and the Western District Conference have given joint support to the church which began in 1982 with Tim Detweiler as pastor. Membership is now 54.

San Antonio, Texas. The San Antonio Mennonite Fellowship was begun in 1984 with Don Reinheimer as pastor. Membership stands at 42.

Fort Worth, Texas. The Hope Mennonite Fellowship was also begun in 1984. The group provided much of its own leadership until the arrival of their first full time pastor, Randy Smith. Current membership is 38.

Boulder, Colorado. Boulder Mennonite Church was started by the Home Missions Committee in 1984 with help from the Arvada Mennonite Church. Marilyn Miller had served as co-pastor at Arvada and was commissioned by the Arvada church to go to Boulder. Arvada and the Western District Conference provided financial help to purchase a meeting house at Boulder. There are 52 members.

Houston, Texas. The Houston Chinese Mennonite Church was begun by the Home Missions Committee in 1985. Peter Lin, a product of General Conference Missions in Taiwan, has been their pastor from the beginning. They have 18 members.

Wichita, Kansas. The Hope Mennonite Church of Wichita was started by the Home Missions Committee, with the First Mennonite Church of Newton as the "mother" church. As in the case of the Salina-Eden mother-daughter relationship, First Mennonite Church provided financial subsidy and other forms of support, such as attendance and Sunday School teachers. Marvin Zehr was the first pastor. Membership now stands at 150.

Austin, Texas. The Austin Mennonite Fellowship began in 1986. As in other cities, Mennonites in Austin began to meet because they experienced the need for fellowship and worship. Kathy Goering Reid is the first full time pastor. Current membership is 44.

Aurora, Colorado. In 1987 the Peace Community Mennonite Church was begun on Denver's east side suburb of Aurora, with Leonard and Joan Wiebe providing pastoral leadership. Representatives of supporting congregations—Arvada, Boulder, First Mennonite, and Glennon Heights—formed a local Denver Area Mennonite Mission Commission which, together with the Home Missions Committee started the congregation. Membership is 67.

Oklahoma City, Oklahoma. The Oklahoma churches, through the Oklahoma Convention, supported by the Home Missions Committee, planted the Joy Mennonite Church in 1987, with Mark Wiens as pastor. There are 20 members.

Dallas, Texas. The Home Missions Committee began a second Spanish-speaking church in Dallas in 1988, with George and Margaret Ediger as pastors. Bethel Mennonite, Inman, Kansas, is the "mother church" and provides financial support. Membership is estimated at 20.

Newton, Kansas. In 1989 the Shalom Mennonite Church was formed with Stanley Bohn as the pastor. This congregation was started with encouragement from the Home Mission Committee and support from both the Faith Mennonite Church and the Bethel College Mennonite Church. The current membership is 79.

Olathe, Kansas. In 1990 the Home Missions Committee and South Central Conference began a church in Olathe, with support of the "mother church," Bethel College Mennonite Church of North Newton. David Whitermore is pastor of the church, New Hope Mennonite, which has a membership of 20.

House churches. Since 1970 five house churches have been established, now having a total of 147 members. These are: Ecumenikos in Kansas City, with 25 members (belonging to four other denominatons) and begun in 1971; New Creation Fellowship in Newton begun in 1973, with 40 current members; Mennonite Church of the Servant in Wichita begun in 1976 with David Habegger as first pastor, now with 30 members; Covenant Mennonite Fellowship begun in Hesston in 1977, with eight current members; Jubilee Mennonite Fellowship in North Newton, begun in 1978, now with 24 members.

Western District Conference and the Home Mission Committee have given encouragement and affirmation to house churches, but have not given substantial funds, except that the Home Missions Committee provided support to David Habegger as pastor at the Mennonite Church of the Servant.

158 Stories of Remembrance & Restoration

Reflections and Conclusions

The nearly 30 congregations planted by the Western District since the 1950s, shows the effort has been an aggressive one. Other evidence of the seriousness of this outreach is the fact that the Home Missions Committee for the last 15 years has employed a half time church planting coordinator to implement its many projects. David Habegger served in that position faithfully for 11 years. Currently Floyd Bartel is coordinator.

The Western District Conference has enthusiastically endorsed church planting by passing resolutions to set church planting goals, and has encouraged financial support from the congregations. At the 1979 conference sessions, for example, the Conference approved a goal to establish 10 new congregations in the next 10 years. The goal was achieved in seven years. Encouraged by this, the Home Mission Committee presented a resolution, approved at the 1986 conference, to establish 15 new congregations in the next 10 years. More recently, however, partly due to lack of funds, church planting has slowed considerably. At the 1991 Conference in Moundridge, the Home Mission Committee reported they now plan for a new church to be planted every other year.

The cost of planting churches is considerable. In the last number of years the Home Missions Committee has made a ten-year financial commitment to the congregations it starts: a full commitment for three years and a phased-down commitment for seven years, based upon the assumption that the church will be self-supporting at the end of ten years. This represents a longer time and a larger amount of support than many other conferences provide for church planting. If we calculate that the 27 congregations planted since the 1950s cost the conference an average of $100,000 each, the total investment exceeds $2.5 million.

Some congregations are begun in cooperation with other conferences, as noted earlier; in these cases Western District cost is less. Nevertheless, the investment is substantial. The current Home Missions Budget is $170,000. To maintain that budget for 10 years would total $1.7 million. In addition, our congregations support the rest of the Western District Conference Budget, which for the current year totals $422,000. We also support General

Conference, Mennonite Biblical Seminary, MCC, CROP/MCC drives, Bethel College, our local congregational budgets and local projects such as nursing homes. It does not take a genius to note that we are spending a lot of money. It does raise the question, specifically with regard to Home Missions church planting: "Is it worth it?" Occasionally there are voices raising the legitimate question: "Are we spending too much money on church planting and not enough in other areas such as peace, hunger, homelessness, and other witness."

There is no sure answer. As a long time worker on several Western District Committees, including Home Missions, I am grateful for the dramatic and exciting period of church planting that we have experienced since 1950 as well as in the first half of the century.

The Western District today includes approximately 80 congregations. Thirty-one of these are congregations planted in the city in this century—27 since 1950. These congregations have a total membership of 3,196. The dollar cost per member may not be really important, but when we consider what our conference would be like without these urban congregations and their membership, we realize how important they are. It would have been a tragedy of great proportions not to have had the church planting outreach effort of this century. We have proved that we can do it. Why should we not be able; our spiritual ancestors were city folks! We thank God that there have been people with commitment and energy to pursue and fulfill our visions. As we thank God for what He has done through and in our district in the past, we pray that the vision and effort will continue. The Western District task in all areas, including church planting, is not finished. In the long view of history, it may only be beginning!

RESOURCES:

Haury, David. 1981. Urbanization and Expansion. In: Prairie People. Newton, KS: Faith and Life Press.

The Sign at Camp Mennoscah
Credit: Loris A. Habegger

A Retreat Center Serves the Conference

THE CAMP MENNOSCAH STORY

by Harley Stucky

The selection and development of Camp Mennoscah is a modern miracle in Western District annals. It's the story of a drama becoming reality. It's not unlike the biblical story of the loaves and the fishes which in the hands of Jesus fed 5,000. It's the story of $642.19 plus a lot of voluntary elbow grease buying land and building on a pay-as-you-go basis to provide an attractive camp for all seasons. It's the story of young people in action. In a way, it's the concluding story of the Young People's Christian Endeavor Fellowship in the Western District.

An idea for a retreat center emerges
The idea of a Western District Retreat emerged in the 1920s when a nine-day retreat was held on the Bethel College campus in 1925. Bethel College continued to host subsequent retreats until 1937 when the retreat site was shifted to Camp Wood, a YMCA camp near Elmdale, Kansas, approximately 50 miles east of Newton. The annual retreats were shifted to Camp Fellowship near Goddard in 1947 and then back to Camp Wood in 1948. Campers who made the trek to Elmdale will never forget the enthusiastic reception by leaders and fellow-campers and the great moments of fellowship and spiritual inspiration. They wanted all Western District young people to have the opportunity for a similar experience.

The desire to develop a Western District camp began in the pre-World War II era. The idea grew and eventually led to Camp Mennoscah. How did this happen? At the August 1945 Western District Christian Endeavor Convention the following resolution was adopted:

Whereas we feel the need for more time for retreats than is allotted to us by Camp Wood, be it resolved that we authorize the Executive Committee to investigate the possibilities of acquiring our own retreat grounds, that they set up a fund for this purpose, and that they enter into negotiations if it seems advisable.

This was the "go-ahead."

A year later, at the 54th annual CE Convention, the Executive Committee reported that they had visited seven potential camp sites and the treasurer reported that $642.19 had come in for the purchase of a retreat ground. The $642.19 in the treasury suggests that it was only by faith and sheer determination that the Committee moved forward. Moreover, the road ahead provided some unique twists and totally unexpected turns! The Executive Committee recommended proceeding with negotiations to purchase 160-175 acres of pasture land in the Flint Hills area at $35-40 per acre. "We believe that this land has genuine possibilities for development and will lend itself well to the purpose for which we intend to use it." The Resolutions Committee went even further at the Convention with the following statement: "Whereas the Executive Committee has recommended plans for the purchasing of the campsite near Cedar Point, be it resolved that we urge wholehearted support of all C.E. societies for this project for financial support, voluntary labor involving such activities as construction of cabins, improvement of grounds, etc."

The Executive Committee also recommended that the C.E. Convention incorporate for the purpose of holding property, that the Christian Endeavor constitution be revised under the guidance of the Education Committee of the Western District and that a separate Retreat Grounds be established. These recommendations proved to be a watershed in Christian Endeavor activity.

Well, why is Camp Mennoscah or the Western District Camp not located at Cedar Point? In the ensuing discussion somebody tabled the resolution of the Executive Committee, stipulated that they continue to investigate potential campsites until the Western District Conference would meet in October 1946, and that the final decision be made at that time with the blessing of the conference.

In the months between August and October the Committee continued to investigate potential campsites. During this period the idea of a camp at Cedar Point was abandoned because the engineer hired to study its soil type reported it would not hold water and it would be impossible to build a lake or pond which the Committee thought essential for a young people's retreat. All eyes shifted to Arlington where there was a complete 20 acre camp for sale. The sale price, rumored to be around $80,000, was far beyond the Western District funding capability. Moreover, the Committee felt it lacked the proper philosophical setting. How could one experience nature and see God as Creator and Father in a tidy, small, man-made facility? The search continued!

A river site is selected
Indecision dragged into 1947 when Ed W. Graber (Eldon Graber's father) from Pretty Prairie pointed out the unique possibilities of a site on the south fork of the Ninnescah River near Murdock, Kansas. The Committee had visited this site before and had been unimpressed. One of them was quoted as saying, "It's only a river embedded in weeds." Mr. Graber pleaded with the Committee to look it over again, noting the river, with a unique 1/2 mile of bedrock, a dam, a ready made farmstead where a director could live, a wilderness of trees and shrubs, some cultivated acres, and the possibility of purchasing another 80 acres on the east side of the river. After considerable discussion the Committee decided to go along with the idea and began negotiating for the 80 acres located largely on the west side of the river. That is how it all began.

The result was the acquisition of the west 80 in early 1948 from Mr. and Mrs. Sam Cole for $8,000. The Coles were delighted to see their land become a church campsite. Conservative, practical-minded Mennonites castigated the committee members for paying such a ridiculously high price for worthless ground. Even W. F. Unruh, who took his wife Pauline and a number of other people to the campsite in 1948 on a hot dry summer day, is reported to have said, as they stepped out of the car into the tall weeds, "This doesn't look like God's country to me."

Now that we had a place, the die was cast. How would we pay for it? What kind of buildings would we need to make it a campsite? How could we make this a place where the presence of God would be felt—a place where young people would catch a vision of abundant life, a life of service, a place where people of all ages would find spiritual refreshment?

The Retreat Program Committee now began to plan for retreats, and this they did in 1949, 1950, and 1951, in the wooded wilderness area of native trees on the west side of the river. Victor Sawatzky, Erwin C. Goering and Harley J. Stucky were retreat directors during those years.

I quote from the 1949 brochure titled Mennonite Western District Conference Retreats:

> 24th Annual Young People's Retreat, August 2-6 and August 8-12, Murdock, Kansas and Second Adult Retreat, August 18-21, Murdock, Kansas. "Draw near to God and He will draw near to you." James 4:8
>
> The purpose of retreat is to help each retreater to know God as Creator, Father, Friend and Jesus Christ as Savior and Lord; to make the teachings of Jesus the pattern for Christian living in all relationships, developing a wholesome balance of the spiritual, mental, social and physical; to develop knowledge, understanding and appreciation of the Bible; to promote active and intelligent loyalty to the Church and to share in its world missionary task; to develop an awareness and appreciation of God's handiwork by living in close contact with nature.

The brochure continues:

> This year we say "camping" because that is exactly what it will be. Camping—among other things—is, briefly, three things: 1) it is living in a nature environment; 2) it is living in a community of people; 3) it implies leadership and guidance. These

three things you will find at the 1949 young people's and adult retreats, which will be held at the new camp site.

There are no buildings on the site and the out-door living will be a new experience for many retreaters. We are asking that local young people's groups bring tents. Some will not be able to provide their own and we are trying to arrange for a pooling of resources in this area. One suggestion is that local groups come to camp in a large truck—cattle truck or the like—bring a large canvas to roof it and use it as sleeping quarters in case of rain. Plans are to have one large tent which can be partitioned and used as kitchen and dining room on one side and sleeping quarters for girls on the other. Retreaters will be asked to help with the kitchen detail. There will be work periods during which campers will help with the camp development program.

We invite all those who would enjoy this kind of experience to come to retreat this year. The Committee wishes for each young person the opportunity to meet God in the out-of-doors and to learn to know Him better in this environment.

Many of the retreaters liked the idea of the independence which came with having their own tents. Of course, adults and counselors worked 26 hour days tightening and loosening camp ropes and checking on campers! There was work to do and all the campers pitched in. As they did the fellowship grew. It was a tremendous experience to live in the woods on the west side of the river, to dry the silverware in sacks on a washline, to have our worship meetings in a tent under the trees, to take showers from water-filled barrels heated by the sun, to wade and stargaze, to live close to nature—those are moments that we who experienced them will never forget. It was a primitive experience, and our young people loved it.

The 80 acres in 1948 became 160 acres in 1949! Why? Since the land on the west side of the Ninnescah was rather low in that wet year of 1949, the rains posed a flood threat to the retreaters. We needed to build the retreat structures on the east side. In 1949, Jacob Lingenfelder and Adam Mueller were sent to Wichita to meet with the owner of the 80 acres located on the east side of the river. They agreed to the purchase price of $4,500. But how do you increase $642.19 to a total of $12,500 to pay for the entire 160 acres? You need an angel in the story to give immediate assistance. A. M. Lohrenz, a dentist in McPherson, saw the vision, gave generously, took a mortgage, and provided the Western District Young People with a plan to pay him as funds came in.

The local C.E. groups got busy raising funds, and when they saw how big the task was, they appealed to the Sunday School, to Mennonite Men, and to the Western District for funds. The Western District Education Committee carried an amount for the retreat as part of its budget.

A name for the grounds

In 1949 no one had heard of Camp Mennoscah. The area was simply referred to as the site for Mennonite Western District retreats at Murdock, Kansas. How did the site become Camp Mennoscah? In 1949 interested persons were invited to submit names for the site. Later, an invitation was extended for all to come to the site on May 14, 1950 to celebrate the 25th anniversary of Western District retreating by coming to help lay the cornerstone for the camp dining hall, and to choose a name for the camp. The Committee had selected three names from those submitted in a contest, and the people in attendance selected Camp Mennoscah. The name combined syllables from *Menno*nite (to indicate that Mennonites had come) with Ninne*scah* (meaning "good river" as named by Indians). In the promotional literature thereafter, the site was referred to as *Camp Mennoscah, Murdock, Kansas*.

The physical development of the campsite took years. In 1948, the Committee spent most of the summer procuring right-of-way to the east side of the river, building a road, testing and drilling for water, extending an electrical powerline to the site, making plans to irrigate the cultivated land areas, and developing policies on fishing and on other uses of the campsite.

Development: a volunteer effort

Developing the campsite took a tremendous amount of time and energy and might never have occurred without numerous benefactors and the help of volunteers from Western District churches. The volunteers were people who caught a vision and were willing to give time and energy to developing the campsite. It began when Olin Ediger, a Wichita engineer, donated a survey of the land; Stanley Regier (son of Reverend J. M. Regier) an architecture student at the University of Kansas, developed a camp design for the east side, noting where buildings might be placed and providing detailed plans for a camp dining hall; Adam Mueller did the walls and roof of the camp dining hall; Dr. Herb Schmidt donated cement blocks for the dining hall; Ernie Unruh, owner and operator of a semi-trailer truck, hauled the blocks to the site; Sam Ediger and his crew donated their time to build the facility. Camp staff were joined by people from Pretty Prairie, Moundridge, Hillsboro, Newton, Goessel, Greensberg, Hanston, and as far away as Deer Creek, Oklahoma, who volunteered their time to build, paint, clean, plumb, fence, or do whatever was necessary to build Camp Mennoscah.

In the period from 1950 to 1952 the large Dining Hall (72x32 feet) was built, with a kitchen (32x40-feet); it included a large fireplace, a project of the First Mennonite Church, Newton. In 1950 and 1951, the Retreat Committee pleaded for concrete platforms for large tents. In early June 1952, a call went out for boys' and girls' cabins to be erected by July 1. Volunteers from Newton and the surrounding area built two cabins (12x20 feet) at the campsite. Volunteers from the Moundridge community built two similar cabins which they moved by truck to the site. Each cabin provided sleeping bunks for eight people. Throughout the 1950s some campers still slept in tents, and many preferred to make tents a permanent part of the camping experience.

In the years that followed, each project and every improvement proposed by the Western District was implemented largely by volunteers. There is no way volunteers can be given enough credit for the development of Camp Mennoscah. They number in the hundreds and deserve appreciation and recognition.

In 1949 there were two Young People's Retreats and one Adult Weekend Retreat. In 1950 an Intermediate Retreat was added to the schedule. In 1951 the schedule expanded further with the addition of a one-day Ministers' Retreat.

In 1952 the retreats were moved to the east side of the river, and a Men's Retreat was added.

In the first two decades of Camp Mennoscah's existence, Christian churches, under the sponsorship of their Kingman church, used the facilities during the month of June, since the Western District did not have a full retreat schedule. After that, Conference retreats and camps of a growing variety filled the calendar for the camping season.

Adam Mueller and his wife Helen served as the first camp directors from 1950-1954. Jake and Helen Lingenfelder had a send-off party for them on April 1, 1950 in North Newton. Dr. J. H. Langenwalter spoke, using verses from Matthew in his own translation of the Great Commission, "We are sending you out as missionaries. Murdock is your station, but the field is much larger than this immediate community. The Muellers are sent to do God's work and to help youth find God in all of life."

After they arrived at the homestead on April 2, 1950, Helen wrote in her diary:

> Everything was unloaded and they were ready for supper by 6:45 p.m. That doesn't mean that we're settled; there is papering yet to do, and an enormous amount of cleanup. In fact we will probably live quite primitive for awhile. Everywhere—in the house, in the farmyard, by the river, on the campsite, things are crying to be done. It will be fine to have a share in the job of camp building. We believe God has called us and we come to do his bidding. It will be a new life for us in this wilderness but we know God is with us.
>
> April 5—What a day! Spent the forenoon with paper, paste and scissors in the kitchen...paper hanging, after a cold lunch...It's hard to know when the master's work is urgent. How one can get it done without rush and panic.

April 11—At about 11:15 a.m. Eddy, Harold and Willard Schrag drove up with a truck load of implements from Moundridge area. While they were unloading, Frank Toews and Alfred Regier drove up with implements from Whitewater. We fed them at noon and then all the men went to the river.

April 12—Another full day! The beginning was eventful because I was planning to do my laundry with tub and washboard. While I was getting things ready, Adam was beginning some planting— Boysenberries or such— and suddenly Harvey Graber chugs onto the yard with his tractor and trailer carrying a plow. The fellows were coming to plow the east 80. Soon three others followed. Adam went with them and they all crossed the river. Three others came in on the east side—seven tractors were part of the pact. They had to burn weeds to keep from jamming up the plows. That caused some excitement because there was just enough wind to let the fire get away sometimes. It wore Adam out, fighting the fire and helping to keep the weeds out of the plows! About 11 a.m. Joe Goering and Jim Zerger drove in with horses. Adam was across the river so I told them to put the critters in the barn.

April 18—John Shay, the game warden from Kingman was here today and went with Adam to estimate damage done by beavers.

April 24— While I was frantically typing this morning, who should show up but the census taker. Adam was plowing so I got him in.

The Muellers were long-suffering and patient and would do everything possible to add to the campers' comfort and retreat enjoyment. Adam used the horses on the farm. He ordered and paid for fruit trees and planted an orchard. The Muellers lived in the red farmhouse and used an outdoor privy. They moved out of the farmhouse November 15, 1954.

Robert and Ruthann (Lichti) Froese served as camp directors from November 1954 to late 1959. Sam Ediger built a kitchen and indoor bathroom in the farmhouse for the Froeses, who were expecting a baby. Their home, still on the west side of the river, was blessed with a son and daughter while they were serving the camp. Robert continued the farming and worked hard with the sprinkler irrigation system, raising alfalfa and keeping weeds out of the orchard. During this period considerable revenue was raised by people who paid a fee for fishing on the west side of the river at Camp Mennoscah.

By July 1, 1952, the dining hall was built, and the retreats were shifted to the east side. Now the Retreat Committee began thinking about a full-time program, needing a staff director, assistant director, cook, assistant cook and someone with skills in crafts. This meant that a facility was needed to house five or six people. The Committee thought the facility should be winterized for all-year programming and should be large enough to accommodate some meetings. The camp staffhouse idea was born. Sam Ediger and his crew built the camp staffhouse, volunteering all of their services. The materials cost over $3,000. During this period wash shelters, tennis courts, softball backstops and a fence around the campsite premises were built. In time the Retreat Committee felt that since the campsite was being developed on the east side, the camp directors' residence should also be constructed there.

The third director and his wife, Mel and Helen Flickinger, (1961-1964) were able to move into a new house on the east side along the road into the camp site. During their term the swimming pool was built, as well as the "A" frame worship center.

Ed and Margaret (Stucky) Thiessen became camp directors in the spring of 1965 and served through 1968. The dining hall was painted and a chapel was built. "Fresh Air Camps" for inner city children also began during this period.

Menno and Mary (Stucky) Doerksen were camp directors from 1968-1974. During these years wings to the north and south of the A-frame worship center were built to accomodate larger meetings. A roof to the west of the dining hall with a storm cellar were added for camper protection.

Bill and Marjorie (Olson) Stucky were directors from 1974-1984. During their period of leadership the swimming pool was rebuilt along with a bathhouse, and a second staffhouse was added.

The first staffhouse was enlarged with bathrooms, and a number of cabins were added, so that there were six boys and six girls cabins. The Work and Play Camp, the Developmentally Disabled Camp, and the Grandparents-Grandchildren Camp came into being.

Richard and Velma Ratzlaff served as directors from 1984 to 1988. They reworked the curriculum and program of most retreats.

Don and Mary Troyer became the camp directors in 1989 and continue in that capacity. Their special interest is nature.

In the late 1950s another major change occurred; a new constitution was written for the Western District young people. In the new constitution the name was changed from Western District Christian Endeavor Fellowship to Youth Fellowship of the Western District. Through all changes, we remember that the inspiration which developed into Camp Mennoscah really came from the Christian Endeavor fellowships which were very strong in our churches in the 1930s and early 1940s. These fellowships included a considerable number of people in high school and college, but they also included people in their midlife years. The young adults were a driving force in the development of Camp Mennoscah. Under the new constitution the Retreat Committee acquired its own identity, on a par with other committees in the Western District Conference.

Representatives on Retreat Committees were from the total Western District, the Western District Education Committee, Mennonite Men, and Women's Missionary Societies. All of these groups working together developed Camp Mennoscah! On the beautiful 160 acres located approximately one mile south and one mile west of Murdock, Kansas, Camp Mennoscah's complete facilities include a beautiful dining hall with extended roof and kitchen overlooking the banks of the Ninnescah River, with a natural rock bottom dividing the camp from the farm. The river provides good fishing and wading. A combination worship and craft center, cabins for campers of all ages, swimming pool and bathhouse, tennis, volleyball, and other recreational courts, a softball diamond and two staffhouses for year-round activities are now a part of an attractive camp built by loving hands of people who cared, who wanted our youth and our adults to have experiences with nature and God. It's a wonderful retreat center. Have you been to Camp Mennoscah lately?

Tried by Fire

EDEN MENNONITE CHURCH OF INOLA, OKLAHOMA

by John W. Voth

"We can move to Oklahoma with our German language, establish farms, and practice our Mennonite beliefs." This is what approximately 15 young families who began the Eden Mennonite of Inola in eastern Oklahoma around 1912 set out to prove. They had come from various places in Kansas, especially Hillsboro and Goessel, leaving behind skeptical relatives who feared they were wasting their family inheritance. Some of them had already attempted and failed to form a new settlement of Mennonites at Syracuse in Hamilton County in western Kansas. Would they be successful in establishing a farming community in Oklahoma? They came expecting to raise wheat like their relatives in Kansas were doing.

Other challenges haunted the minds of these young families. Would they be able to worship God as they wanted? Would their children grow up to believe and follow Jesus Christ? How would they be accepted by the community? The children had already found that their German language was a cause for conflict in school.

By 1914, N. J. Hiebert and J. P. Remple had donated $50 each to buy a school building which was converted into a church. The building was moved and set up with an entrance to the south on land donated by Henry Pankratz. The present church is at this same location. The church was formally organized on November 12, 1914, and joined the General Conference in 1915. Their settlement was beginning to look somewhat secure.

The people of Eden had their share of testing. The land was not suitable for raising large crops of wheat with the farming methods of the time. Many of them found it hard to get credit, and crop failures seemed to plague them. Their biggest test, however, came with the advent of World War I.

Their first pastor was Herman Jantzen from Stanton County, Kansas. Solomon Mouttet was elected to share in the ministry. On July 24, 1918, the Solomon Mouttet family experienced the stillborn death of a baby. That same day the baby was buried in the church cemetery. John and Willie Voth, two brothers who were neighbors to the Mouttet family, missed the service because they were shocking wheat at the Mouttet place.

Another tragedy was about to strike. That same evening a family near the church saw an unusual glow in the darkening sky. Their church was burning!

Ten-year-old Anna Voth (later, Pankratz) had attended the graveside service of the Mouttet baby that day. When she and her family saw the fire they hurried to the church. Anna remembers the sinking feeling she had as she witnessed the church's burning.

What caused the fire? Rumor was that the fire had been deliberately set. Waldo Funk's family lived one mile south of the church. He tells how as a young child he watched the scene from home. "It was scary to think that one's neighbors would burn down the church."

But why would anyone burn the church of these Mennonite families? As newcomers the Mennonites posed a threat to the community in several ways.

Their ambitious plans to plow up the meadows and ranch land to turn them into wheat fields was upsetting to some. The community had an image of itself and who its most successful farmers and citizens were. It also had an image of how farming ought to take place in this community which the Mennonites were threatening to change.

On the other hand the Mennonites did not make much effort to develop public relations. Most of them were young, poor, German-speaking, and not well educated at the time. They were fearful of mixing with their "English" neighbors. As a result they were reticent in relating their background or beliefs. The English-speaking people saw them as "standoffish;" they felt these people were anti-American rather than just people with a different culture.

Because of the war with Germany, neighbors were suspicious of anyone who spoke German. After all, were not these American neighbors sending their sons across the ocean to fight Germans? Who would fight the Germans in their own back yard? Rumors were around, possibly rightly so, that these Germans were writing to people in Germany. It seemed logical to conclude that secrets were being communicated to the German government.

Not only did these Mennonites speak German, but some of their members refused to go into military service. During World War I the government had no developed policy on alternative service for people with convictions against going to war. Many of those who were drafted from Eden chose to be noncombatant, not a popular position. Jake Janzen from the Eden Church was court-martialed and incarcerated at Fort Leavenworth, Kansas.

One night Willheim Berg was kidnapped from his home. His grieving wife called on the Henry Froese family three miles north of the church. Willheim returned home a few days later. His captors had stuffed his pockets full of Red Cross buttons and war bonds. The Red Cross was closely associated with the military at the time. He wouldn't talk about who took him or what happened.

Not everyone in the community saw the Mennonites as a threat. Many neighbors had grown to love and respect them. A local grocery owner said they were the best at paying their bills. Many neighbors were appalled that someone would burn the Mennonite Church. Yet the invisible threat was scary.

What would this conflict do to this young Mennonite community? The little group was determined not to give up. Anna Voth's father, G. J. Voth, invited the church to meet in his barn. The Voth family had just completed a new house in the spring. During the building of the house the family had lived in two grain bins in the barn. Many of the family belongings were still in the barn. The church started meeting in the haymow of this barn.

John Funk, Jake Martins, Art Heibert, and Henry Froese were baptized in this barn. The church met there about five weeks until, on September 8, the barn also was set on fire and burned to the ground. Fortunately, the horses had been taken out of the barn to pasture earlier that evening. George and his son John tried to get a new wagon out of a lean-to on the north side of the barn. John remembers fire falling on them as they strained to get the wagon out. Finally they had to give up and let it burn. That same day the local Mennonite Brethren church was destroyed by fire.

What kind of feeling must have been going through the Eden members? Anna Voth remembers the barn fire as an "utter horror" as she watched from an upstairs window of the house. Many of their household goods had been destroyed. She remembers thinking that if "they," the "German haters," hated them so much as to set fires, they would surely do awful things to a ten-year-old girl.

After the crisis was over, Anna's mother decided to learn a positive lesson from this fire. Shortly after her marriage she and her husband G. J. Voth had homesteaded in a dug-out in Western Kansas. Such living conditions just didn't seem the proper place to use some of her best wedding gifts so she kept them packed away. In Oklahoma, she had planned to unpack those precious things when they moved into the new house, but they were still packed away in the barn and were destroyed in the fire. Later Anna's mother would often repeat this story, concluding with an admonition: "Use and enjoy what you have. Don't spend your life fretting about storing things away." When she died her family had very little "junk" to sort through.

What effect did these fires have on the church community? According to G. B. Regier, a long-time pastor of Eden who farmed to make his living, the congregation was not adversely affected at all. In fact, the trouble drew the congregation together and united them.

The barriers with the community gradually broke down, and today Eden has good relationships with the community. Members became active in community projects like conservation. They became local school teachers and business leaders. Today the church has several members with nonethnic names who have joined the church and married into the church families. God is giving Eden an opportunity to share God's love in a community that was at one time hostile to it.

RESOURCES:

"Burial, Burnings, Buttons, and Bonds" by Robert C. Coon in *The Mennonite*, Oct. 11, 1988, pp. 435-436.

AUTHOR BIOGRAPHIES

Lois Duerksen Deckert grew up in India where her parents, Jacob R. and Christina Harder Duerksen were missionaries. She graduated from Bethel College with a bachelor's degree in Education. She and her husband, Marion, worked for MCC in Akron, Pennsylvania, Morocco and Indonesia. They moved to North Newton in 1972 when Marion took a job at Bethel College. Lois edited *Window to Mission*, the magazine for General Conference Women in Mission, for seven years. She enjoys gardening, reading, writing, cooking and watching birds. Lois and Marion have two grown children, Alan and Alice, a son-in-law, Mike McGrath and a granddaughter, Caitlin Elizabeth. Lois and Marion are members of the Bethel College Mennonite Church.

Bertha Fast Harder was born in Mountain Lake, Minnesota. She taught first grade and worked with Mennonite Central Committee in refugee camps in Egypt and Italy. Bertha graduated from Mennonite Biblical Seminary and was an instructor in the seminary for 25 years. She participated in planning and writing the Foundation Series Curriculum. She now lives in North Newton, Kansas, with her husband, Leland. The Harders have two sons and two granddaughters. Bertha is active in Christian education in the Bethel College Mennonite Church and in the Western District. She also serves as a docent at Kauffman Museum.

James C. Junhke teaches history at Bethel College and is a member of the Bethel College Mennonite Church. He has written a number of books and dramas about Mennonite history. From 1958 to 1960, he served with the MCC-Pax program in Germany. From 1971 to 1973 he was MCC director in Botswana. In 1988-1989 he was an exchange teacher in China under the China Education Exchange. He is married to Anna Kreider Juhnke. They have two children, Joanne and Karl.

Marlene Krehbiel and her husband, Maynard, live on a farm near McPherson, Kansas. Their four adult children are married and established in their own homes. The Krehbiels have four grandchildren. When their youngest son was in junior high, Marlene entered college for the first time. Another childhood dream was fulfilled when she graduated four years later with a teaching degree. Since then (1982) she has been teaching English, German, and speech at Inman High School, Inman, Kansas. The Eden Mennonite Church of Moundridge has always been her church home. Through the years, Marlene has taught Sunday school and served in various other ways—the most humbling and challenging one was being elected to serve as the first deaconess in 1988.

Tim Lehman is a product of First Mennonite Church, Berne, Indiana. He was educated in Mennonite schools—Goshen College and Associated Mennonite Biblical Seminaries. He has served as Program Director at Camp Friedenswald in Michigan, and continues his strong interest in Christian camping by heading a northern Minnesota camping ground. His wife, Paula, was secretary of Youth Education for several years. Tim pastored at Eden Mennonite Church for several years before he and his family took up full time work in Minnesota camping. He maintains a strong interest in Mennonite and Anabaptist history and churches.

Wilma Entz McKee grew up in the Bethel Mennonite Church, Hydro, Oklahoma. Her education includes a master's degree in guidance and counseling from Southwestern Oklahoma State University. She taught in public schools for 36 years, retiring in 1990. She has served on retreat, education and home missions committees for Oklahoma Convention and Western District Conference. At present Wilma is a member of the General Conference historical committee and is the author of *Heritage Celebrations: A Resource Book for Congregations*, sponsored by the historical committee. Her other writing includes: editing and contributing writer of *Growing Faith: General Conference Mennonites in Oklahoma* (Faith and Life Press, 1988) and *The Valued Child: Natural Development Allows for Success* (Self-published,

1990). At this time she is involved in writing, tutoring, and counseling.

Walt Neufeld is a native of Inman, Kansas and a son of the Bethel Mennonite Church, Inman. He is a graduate of Mennonite schools —Bethel College and Mennonite Biblical Seminary. His pastoral ministry provided leadership for Hillsboro First Mennonite, Eden Mennonite (Moundridge), Ransom-Hanston congregations in Kansas, and Wayland Mennonite in Iowa. He has held conference offices and continues to be a strong supporter of peace, voluntary service, and home missions. As a retired pastor, Walt has served in interim capacities. He is an avid auto mechanic and used car salesman. He and his wife, Frieda, live in Moundridge. They are the parents of three sons, three daughters and several grandchildren.

Rosella Wiens Regier's childhood home and her church, Bethel Mennonite Church, were in the Inman, Kansas, area. Currently she and her husband, Harold, are members of the Faith Mennonite Church, Newton, Kansas. She is the Executive Director for *Jubilee: God's Good News,* a new Anabaptist Sunday school curriculum project; she works with 150 persons from six denominations in the effort. She has been a General Conference mission worker in Gulfport, Mississippi, a public school teacher in Kansas, Indiana, and Mississippi, the secretary and vice-president of the Western District, and a staunch supporter of conference educational ventures in many areas. She enjoys gardening, antiques, the ocean, relationships, reading, and family trips. The Regiers are parents of a son and a daughter.

Maynard Shelly, Newton, Kansas, a former editor for the General Conference Mennonite Church, served as secretary of the Western District Peace and Social Concerns Committee, 1974-1980. He continues to write Sunday school curriculum and church history. He is a member of the Bethel College Mennonite Church.

Harley J. Stucky, born in Moundridge, Kansas, was involved in camping and young people's activities from 1937 to the 1960s. He attended Camp Wood at Elmdale and served as camp director at Camp Mennoscah in 1950 and 1951. He served on the Western District Education Committee and was advisor to the Retreat and Camp Planning Committee. Harley helped write the new constitution for WDC young people in the early 1950s and the job descriptions for the various commmittees involved in developing Camp Mennoscah. He taught history and political science at Bethel College and served as Vice President of Academic Affairs and Dean and Registrar at Friends University. He has a Ph.D. from Northwestern University.

John Wesley Voth, son of John J. and Ella Rempel Voth, grew up in the Eden Mennonite Church, Inola, Oklahoma. He is a graduate of Grace College of the Bible and Dallas Theological Seminary and has studied at Mennonite Biblical Seminary. He was minister of the Immanuel Mennonite Church, Delft, Minnesota, for 11 years and served the New Hopedale Mennonite Church, Meno, Oklahoma, for eight and one-half years. Since 1990, John has served the Eden Mennonite Church, Inola, Oklahoma.

David C. Wedel was born in Goessel, Kansas, in 1908. He received a B.A. degree from Bethel College in 1933, a B.D. degree from Colgate-Rochester Divinity School in 1936, and a Th.D. degree from Iliff School of Theology in 1952. David served as pastor of the First Mennonite Church, Halstead, Kansas, from 1936 to 1946; president of Bethel College from 1952 to 1959; Associate Director of Development at Southwestern College from 1959 to 1967; and in the department of Alumni and Church Relations, Bethel College, from 1967 to 1975. After his retirement in 1975 until 1984, David served as Interim Pastor for six churches. He lives in North Newton with his wife, Martha.